She's a Keeper!

Cockamamie Memoirs from a Hot Southern Mess

by

Lee St. John

To my family: present and past.

Thanks for tolerating me. I know it hasn't been easy.

Acknowledgments

I'd like to acknowledge Pinterest and thesaurus.com.
I couldn't have done it without you.

Table of
Contents

1. Rubber Ducky
2. Don't You Believe It
3. Who Can it Be Knocking at My Door?
4. Do Not Try This at Home?
5. "I've Got the Wedding Bell Blues?"
6. Dick Tracy
7. The More You Drink, the Better I Look
8. *S'il vous plaît excusez-moi*
9. Rain, Rain Go Away
10. "I'm Larry; this is my Brother, Daryl, and my other brother, Daryl"
11. Corndog Sticks
12. "Who's Been Sleeping in My Bed?"
13. Presidential Pets
14. Dag Nab It!
15. Serenity Now
16. You've Come a Long Way, Baby!
17. A Brave New World
18. A Hurricane by Any Other Name May Not Sound So Sweet
19. I Am Not Sweet

20. Pride Goeth Before a Fall
21. Boo!
22. Name Calling
23. Live and Learn
24. Gumption
25. Jive Talking
26. I Feel Bad About My Neck, Too
27. It's a *Wonder* the Relationship Lasted this Long
28. The Customer is Always Right
29. How Do You Spell F***?
30. One Tomato, Two Tomato, Three Tomato, *More*!
31. The Husband's Guide to Marriage by Lewis Grizzard
32. Big Mack
33. Must-See TV!
34. What Were You Expecting?
35. The Royal Wedding
36. A Little Dab Will Do Ya
37. Kissin' Cuzins
38. Sentimental Journey
39. Toot, Toot
40. Vivisepulture
41. F – Failure or Fantastic? You Decide
42. Grading Papers
43. Take Me Out to the Ballgame
44. I Am a *Sucker*!
45. I Am a Tooth Grinder
46. I Don't Want to Grow Up
47. You Better Watch Out, You Better Not Cry…
48. Secret Agent
49. "Miss Right" or "Miss Right Now"?
50. Bonjour!
51. Tales from the Crypt

52. Do Not Call Me. I'll Call You.
53. Bobcats, and Cougars, and Bears. Oh, My!
54. Microeconomics 101
55. Sometimes I Give Myself the Creeps
56. The Family Jewels
57. The Purloined Letter?
58. Testing, Testing
59. Do You Pass Muster?
60. "I Can't Take it Anymore!"
61. Spoiled Rotten
62. Brain Fog – Everyone Needs a Mrs. Wiggins!
63. I'm a KD Lady
64. Acting Presidential
65. Senioritis
66. Senioritis, part 2
67. 280 Characters
68. The Augusta Masters
69. What's Your Excuse?
70. "Boom!" Says Auburn Coach Gus Malzahn
71. Paper Trail
72. "She Wore an Itsy Bitsy Teenie Weenie Yellow Polka Dot Bikini"
73. When I'm Sixty-Four
74. The Tooth Fairy
75. Dam It!
76. Letter to the Editor
77. Whatever Works
78. "I Don't Know Nothin' 'bout Birthin' Babies," said Prissy
79. Love It or Leave It
80. The Shadow Knows
81. The "Me, too" Movement
82. A Hot Tamale vs. A Bean Counter

83. First Fight?
84. "I am Groot!"
85. Be Careful What You Wish For
86. When the Stars Aligned
87. Bon Voyage!

Rubber Ducky

*H*ubby and I have two sons who are eight years apart. It's like having two only children. When our oldest graduated from high school and went to college, our youngest was just entering fifth grade. Yes, the younger one played tag-a-along pretty much with the eldest's extra-curricular sport endeavors. The eldest got out of attending his younger sibling's games and performances somewhat because he was away at college. He went a few times but he was busy with his own rigorous demands.

I had such a dichotomy in those two at the same time. I jokingly told my friends while one was getting his baby teeth, the other was losing his. When one was beginning to talk, the other was learning to talk back. One wanted to follow his older brother everywhere and that older brother wanted to be left alone. You get the picture. Two different worlds. Like in Superman's Bizzaro World, which in popular culture means a situation or setting which is weirdly inverted or opposite to expectations.

And eight years makes a difference when you talk about advancement in baby gadgets. We thought we were getting along just fine with the inventions the The Heir used, but when The Spare arrived—I was influenced by the British media's nicknames for William and Harry—caring for a new baby was so much easier! There were many more creative tools, mechanisms, and toys to help make my life smoother.

With the first child, we had the best of everything ever offered to a baby. We had the cutest handmade cross-stitched bib; hand-stitched Feltman rompers with Peter Pan collars and shorts with decorative buttons closure at the waist; embroidered and monogrammed pillows and sheets; high-priced toys from Toys-R-Us, and such. His room had Boykin's Bears designed window treatments more expensive than curtains in our own bedroom. Our Amish wooden high chair was no different. Do you know how hard it was to clean caked-on food from the wood on that high chair? The slats were the worst. I should have just gotten one with the plastic tray. But, ohhh, nooo! We had to have the top-of-the-line *everything* for our first child.

Dropping a pacifier on the ground was certainly a biggie for your first prodigy, as you either boiled it later to sterilize it before using it again or, worse, just threw it away. Germs! No three-second rule. It was damaged goods. You'd better have brought a ton of passies with you everywhere you went because they were eventually going to fall out of your baby's mouth at the most inopportune times.

The sippy cup hadn't changed much since the 1950s, and in 1986 was still a hard plastic ball cut in half with a spout on top that twisted off and had handles on each side of the bottom half. After filling it with juice, you screwed the spout part to the bottom half handle part and hoped your child never dropped it. Well, that didn't happen. They dropped it, they threw it, they stepped on it, or they kicked it. The top part popped off from this wear and tear and there was sticky spilled juice all over the kitchen floor. *Yuck!*

But all that changed by the time The Spare arrived. A new and improved modern sippy cup had a mechanism that used springs which held the top on better, and when dropped, the top of the cup stayed on and didn't cause a mess. I *loved* it! I was more relaxed with the second child, too. If his pacifier dropped on the ground, I just wiped it against my slacks and stuck that sucker right back in from where it fell out. Dirt has nutrients, right?

And I solved my messy high chair dinner situation, too. Wasn't bath time always after dinner? I learned a new trick. I placed The Spare in the tub to eat his dinner. Yep, right in the tub. It was a contained mess. Afterward, I just sprayed and washed him off. Problem solved. It was a two-fer!

But I did worry later that because he ate so many meals in the tub during bath time—sometimes I just put him in the tub to feed him even if I wasn't giving him a bath—that like the conditioning of Pavlov's dog, when The Spare grew up, he might feel hungry and crave food every time he bathed and he'd wonder why.

Don't You Believe It

*A*s an only child, I had all the elderly mother caretaker privileges by myself. I say privilege because it was something I was happy to do, although it was sad at the same time. My mother and father were forty when I was born, and so my world was hanging around with their older friends. Had I been born to a mother who was twenty, my own parents could have been my grandparents. My friends' mothers and fathers were anywhere from ten to fifteen years younger than mine. They were youthful and energetic while I visited their homes. Mine? Not as much.

I always worried that my parents would pass away long before any of my friends' parents did. But that was not the case. I had mine for a lengthier time than I expected.

My father passed away first. After my mother died, it soon became time for my friends to have a taste of what it was like to care for their aging parents. Some of them had to decide on nursing homes, hospitals, and assisted living locations. When my mother was still living in her own home after Daddy died or was staying at her retirement facility, I remember how nice it was for someone outside the family to take the time to visit her in her later years. I wanted to pay back that nice gesture.

Because so many of these elderly individuals were living in the same nursing home facility in my small town, I visited three or four octogenarians all in one trip. I called it my Geriatric Run. I was used to having conversations with older people because of my mother and father's age group, so I enjoyed these social calls. My own great-aunts and uncles were in the mix for visitation day. Slowing down but still aware, they bequeathed to me years earlier a beautiful pair of sterling silver candlesticks that once belonged to my grand-parents. They wanted to place these keepsakes with a family member who would take care of them in the future. The candlesticks were engraved with a single initial, an A, from my grandparents' surname. And, of course, by having them displayed on my dining room table, I fondly remember these special relatives.

One day after visiting a friend's parent in the nursing home, I walked down the hall toward the entrance, first having to pass by the patients' bedroom apartments. In this corridor was one of the sweetest-looking women I had ever seen. Strolling slowly, I was about to catch up with her, and it was then I noticed her sparkling ice blue eyes and her completely gorgeous white hair. She looked like an angel. She smiled at me and I wondered if she really was an angel. Then she spoke and said, "Hello," and her voice had such melody I took a liking to her instantly.

Before I could return her greeting, this Wacko-Wicked-Witch-Of-The-West-type woman appeared, walking fast, and was about to catch up to us. This scrawny, uncombed, straw-like, wild-haired hag with a scowl on her face spoke as she pointed to the beauty next to me and said in a raspy, scratchy voice as she passed us, "She's been cussing at me all day and calling me names."

First, I thought, *How did I get pulled in to this nursing home drama?* And second, it just could *not* be true because my new friend was as adorable as she could be with the sweetest eyes and doll face, while the other wretched woman transmitted, "Do Not Touch." One represented demure, genteel, and proper behavior, while the other appeared crass, rude, and offensive. The ugly woman's harsh voice continued, "I mean it. Calling me names all day!"

The sweetheart next to me lowered her head, looked up shyly, and said timidly in her little-girl soft voice, "I have not. I don't know what she's talking about."

I looked in her eyes and said gently, "I understand. I am sure you didn't. I don't know why she thinks I am interested in hearing that. I really don't want to get involved. Let's just ignore her."

The loud and crude woman walked on ahead of us in a huff, made a quick turn into her room, but left her apartment door open. The darling woman and I walked together a few steps down the hall, but as I had to depart, I started to walk a little faster. I was not yet out of earshot when I realized the beauty of the nursing home was apparently passing by the biddy's apartment because I had to turn and see for myself what it was I heard. That angel had directly stopped by her adversary's room and yelled, "Bitch!"

Here was yet was another reminder you *do not* judge a book by its cover.

Who Can It Be Knocking at My Door?

*W*ho was this family I married into? Their mantra was, "If you ever gather four Episcopalians together in one room, you are bound to find a fifth." And in this case, they were so right.

Two years into our marriage, our first child was born. I was an only child, but Hubby's family consisted of an elder brother and sister, although they were both single and had no children. Hubby's parents were also older when he was born. So our boisterous toddler was the first grandchild in a group of adults advanced in age, all who either knew nothing about caring for a tot or had forgotten how.

While visiting his sister's Alabama home in a condominium community, Hubby's parents, his brother, and my family enjoyed her neighborhood's pool. The Heir splashed and giggled the entire time as we watched with delight. When it was time to leave and start dinner, I asked all the adults would they mind if I was excused so that I could take a shower and wash my hair. All five pairs of peeps were fine with it. They would keep an eye out for this first-born golden child of theirs. I told them it wouldn't take longer than thirty minutes.

"Think you can handle it?" I asked.

"Of course," they all replied while pouring their five-o'clock-somewhere whiskey.

And thirty minutes later, I hurriedly dried off and dressed to join the others and see how everything was going with the toddler-sitting. I walked into the kitchen where everyone had red cheeks and were in a jovial mood since it was cocktail hour despite them being at it for a while. Looking around the room and seeing only adults, the first thing out of my mouth was, "Where is The Heir?"

I then saw the fear on all their faces as they looked at each other, turned pale, then looked at me in horror. At that horrible moment when I saw their reaction to my question, they realized that not one of them had been watching the progeny. Frightened, I processed what I had worried might happen—*no one* was keeping an eye on our son and now he was *missing*! With that thought still lingering in my brain, there was a knock at the partially open patio sliding glass door. A woman was outside holding our only child's hand, asking if he belonged to us. She had found him at the pool gate trying to get back in, and since there was no identification on him, she had been going door to door to the closest neighbors to discern to whom he might belong.

If there had been a second more of uncertainly about where he was, I would have fainted.

Five adults were so busy catching up with each other's lives during the cocktail hour and not being used to having a child underfoot that they hadn't a clue how to make a plan of someone being in charge. Who was this family I was stuck with? I never, *ever* let that child out of my sight again whenever they were around...until he turned eighteen.

Do Not
Try This
at Home?

I am not a dentist. Although I have been a regular on a morning TV show on Alabama's Charter Cable, I do not play a dentist on TV. I just play one at home. And I promise you I can save you some money for yourself or your children. You dentists out there reading this, stop now. You don't want to know the information I am passing on to the readers.

I don't fear dentists now, but as a little girl growing up, my hometown dentist was terrifying. If you are of a certain generation like I am—they call us Baby Boomers—you will remember that dentists also worked on Saturdays. Mother was a teacher and I was in school, so, except for the summers, we made one of our twice a year dental appointments on Saturdays during the school year.

This hometown dentist, probably in his mid-fifties, had dark hair and bushy eyebrows. I was already afraid of him and it didn't help that Mother said he was not well as he had a stomach ailment that caused his lower torso—which was leaning in close to my ear as he worked in my mouth—to erupt in a cacophony of intestinal sounds. She tried her best to help me get over this fear of him using a diversion tactic. She's take me out to lunch before our cleaning. There wasn't much in the way of eating out in our county in the early 1960s, so we stopped for a BBQ sandwich and Brunswick stew at a local joint.

Mother always suggested I get my cleaning done first to get it over with. That was a good thing. When my appointment was over, I'd sit in his lobby reading *Highlights* magazine waiting on Mother. But this Saturday was worse than usual. Because of his illness, he remained miserable, and made me miserable by yelling at me a lot and telling me to "Breath through your nose. Breathe through your nose!" Yeah, that was going to help me relax. When he yelled one too many times, which upset me, I threw up on him. He then knew what I had eaten for lunch.

But I digress.

It wasn't until I was an adult that my fear of dentists left me as I found another one whose entire office made one feel relaxed. I inherited my mother's diastema, which is the space between your front teeth caused by the muscle behind them. Mother's and mine were on the upper front two teeth. I wanted to rid myself from this Alfred-E.-Newman-*Mad-Magazine*-cover gap. The rest of my teeth were perfectly straight. I never had to wear braces and only had a few cavities. One dentist told me once, "You are not going to help me pay for my dental practice." Dentists, if you are still reading, you've been warned. I am about to explain why I was not a great billable unit.

First, I had help from a high school classmate who did wear braces. This fellow student contributed daily two rubber bands from his elastic band collection. While we sat in our French I classroom, an hour-long class, he gave me two bands which I placed around my four front teeth. Thinking if I just wrapped my front two teeth, I'd cause another gap somewhere else in my pearly white lineup. I wore the elastic bands around my upper incisors and after two weeks, the gap closed.

Let's do the math: one hour a day x ten school days = zero dollars.

Second lesson is a little trickier. When I told my students

this story, because they were underage, I referred to my long neck glass container as a Coca-Cola bottle. But since you all are over the drinking age, you know what that amber bottle was in reality. Let's begin from the top: I was in an establishment that served ice-cold foamy refreshments in tall bottles. While holding this brew in my right hand, I was just about to take a swig, when someone pushed by me and hit my right elbow, causing the long neck glass container to bump into my left front tooth. Hurting, I rubbed my tongue over the spot and realized there was a crevice along the bottom edge.

When I returned home, I looked in my bathroom mirror and saw the crescent-shaped gap, although small, in my front tooth where just the hour before there wasn't one. OMGosh! Now what? I took matters into my own hands, as always, and found my angel hair nail file and...why not? I was already numb. I had to be careful not to file too much off so as to keep it pretty even with the twin tooth...or hit a nerve.

Don't let your dentist know about these dental tips. I am trying to help you out here by obviously saving the big bucks for such little problems. I mean, I've been figuring out my own teeth dilemmas for years and I am happy to share. At this moment, I've lost my tooth-grinding protector and am using a pacifier. So, there's your third lesson. Those tooth guards are expensive.

You're welcome.

"I've Got the Wedding Bell Blues?"

This is either a fairy tale or a nightmare.
Once Upon a Time…

No one said a thing. The bride asked over and over, "What time is it now?" The answers came back continuously, "Just a few minutes since you last asked."

It was her wedding day. She dressed in the Brides Room of a small Presbyterian Church with her five bridesmaids. She was almost thirty years old and had dreamed of this day for a long time. The groom was also thirty. It was their first marriage.

The reception was going to be held at the bride's family home in their front yard this second Saturday in May. The flowering bushes and potted flora placed throughout the landscape were identical in color to the bridesmaids' dresses: Rubrum lily magenta. Their dresses were made from American Beauty taffeta with a fitted bodice and portrait neckline that had cap sleeves and a longer back hemline. Her attendants carried Rubrum lily bouquets in the same color to match their dresses. The bride wore a candlelight white dress of ivory satin and French re-embroidered lace. The bodice of the gown was pearled Alencon lace which featured a deeply scooped neckline and had tiny puffed sleeves. The skirt fell from a natural waistline and swept back into a chapel-length train. A deep border of Alencon lace edged the gown and train.

The bride's headpiece had a wreath of satin roses and forget-me-nots to which the chapel-length veil of illusion tulle was attached. Streamers of satin ribbons trailed from the back of the wreath headdress. Influenced by the grandeur of Lady Diana Spencer's bouquet on her wedding day, she carried a large all-white bouquet of gardenias—her favorite flower—along with tube roses and stephanotis, with cascading ribbons matching the color of her dress. Both the headpiece and gown were purchased at Regenstein's in Atlanta and were securely packed in a box for safekeeping after the wedding. Still in her closet, the dress hasn't seen the light of day for over thirty-five years.

The groom and his ushers wore grey tuxes and tails for this mid-afternoon wedding.

And here it was, this beautiful day, and the ceremony hadn't started. And what was the time again? There were a few hushed and frantic whispers in the dressing room. The bride noticed her bridesmaids left the room repeatedly, but what she didn't know was these bridesmaids were snatching snippets on the reason for the ceremony's delay. The action was happening outside the church grounds, on the bridge over the expressway, anywhere but in the church's sanctuary. Rumor had it that the groom had vanished and his future mother-in-law was on his tail. Was he going to be a runaway groom?

The congregation was getting antsy as well because that's all they knew, too. The groom now was driving his future-mother-in-law's car, with her sitting in the front seat beside him. They were like bats out of hell heading out of town. What just happened?

While the groom, his best man, and his groomsmen were mentally preparing for the service to begin, the minister casually asked the groom for the marriage license so it could be signed before the ceremony. He did not have it with him. It was in the glove compartment of his car, which was parked and hidden in the basement garage—so as not to be found and tampered with—at the bride's home where the reception was to take place. The minister refused to start the ceremony without this legal document being signed.

Luckily, one of the guests at the wedding was the city's chief of police. He got on his dispatch and notified all the city's police officers and even the county's deputies, since the chase would change jurisdictions, to allow a lime green Delta 88 to pass through the town and the county without being stopped for speeding. Once the document was retrieved, a small police escort with flashing lights and blaring sirens again cleared the highway from the bride's home back to the church so as not to make the ceremony start any later that it already was.

The congregation and bridesmaids did not know the whole story of escape, and capture, and thought something was amiss. So, when the groom finally walked into the sanctuary with his best man about thirty minutes late, the attendees gave a loud collective sigh of relief, then nervously laughed, and clapped when he finally showed up.

The prince hadn't abandoned his princess, and thirty-five years later…a happily ever after.

The Beginning...

Dick Tracy

What is it they say about only children? I've heard it all about the characteristics of only children, of which I am one. But I never heard this. According to the *Independent*, "…different family environments—growing up with or without siblings—does affect children's structural brain development, researchers claim." And this study further claims that "…only children who performed higher on creativity actually showed a higher volume of gray matter in the parietal lobe—a part of the brain associated with mental flexibility and imagination."

So that's where it's coming from.

Learning to keep myself entertained as an only child, I once pretended I was a piano teacher. I started playing the piano when I was in the third grade. I took lessons for nine years so I had stacks of old practice music lying around or in my piano bench. Around fifth grade, I pulled out my own previous beginner lesson practice books and used them to teach my student, who even had a name: Becky Rogers. Like my piano teacher, I wrote her name at the top of my old piano books. If you took piano, you probably remember the red-covered John Thompson music books. I still have several.

Becky Rogers was a poor student. To help her develop better as a pupil, I wrote in the most unrefined handwriting to "pianissimo" on a certain part of a piano piece that she was playing for me, or I wrote other such music verbiage on the music in the book. Becky must not have practiced very much, because there sure was a *lot* of my third-grade scrawled instructions as her teacher on the sheet music about how to play her piece better. I even had a spiral notebook just like my music teacher's where she took notes for me on the pieces I played for her during my instruction and what I should practice for the next lesson. Honestly, I didn't like practicing either. I get it, Becky Rogers. I guess it was more like, "Do as I say, not as I do."

In my younger years, I pretended I was Dale Evans. I had the entire cowgirl outfit. My down-the-street neighbor was Roy Rogers. He was just a year older than me when we played Dale and Roy around the age of four and five. I ran down to his house and rang the front doorbell, his mother would answer and I asked, "Can Roy come out to play?"

I was dressed in Dale's solid red shirt with a plaid kerchief and a faux suede jacket with fringe. There was a round skirt and I kept a holster around my waist for my toy gun. I wore white majorette boots. My cowgirl hat was tan and I wore tan gloves so I wouldn't chap my hands while riding my horse, Buttermilk. My childhood friend dressed similar to Roy, well, as best he could. I am sure he didn't put as much effort into it as I.

When The Heir dressed up around the age of four, his imagination consisted of Popeye, Robin Hood, Superman, or Dick Tracy. I even let him wear his costumes to the grocery store or other public places. People greeted him and said something like, "Hi there, Superman!" or whoever he was that day.

One time while dressed as Dick Tracy, I tried to figure out what to do with him that day, so I took him to the city's police station. When we walked inside, I looked directly into the eyes of the lady at the front desk, all the while shaking my head in the negative, and asked her, "Is Dick Tracy here today?" I had to ask twice because, at first, she didn't understand my questioning and where I was going with it, but seeing mini-Dick Tracy, she put two and two together while I shook my head for her realize I wanted her to say no. She did.

"Why, uh, no, he isn't," she said.

"But he does have a desk here, right? I mean, his desk is in his office here even though he is not available?" This time she got my drift as I nodded in the affirmative behind my son's back.

"Why, yes, he has an office here. I can show you where he works," she commented as she pointed to a closed door.

And when she opened the door, there sat an empty desk with papers scattered all over it as though someone was busy at work and had been called away in a rush. I turned to our oldest and said, "See, honey? Dick Tracy is out catching criminals and isn't at his desk. He's very busy. We tried."

If you are looking for something to do, maybe on a rainy day to make it fun but doesn't cost money…just entertain your child or grandchild by taking them someplace that doesn't really exist, make up a story that one day you can retell or write about to embarrass your children…or yourself.

The More
You Drink, the Better
I Look

When I was a senior in college, I was enrolled in a university not far from the Atlantic Ocean beaches. This was my last fall at school and my parents wanted to visit me. It was a four-hour drive from my hometown and my roommates and I really didn't have a place for them to stay over. My parents and I decided on a trip away from my campus and so they swung by, picked me up, and then we headed to Hilton Head, South Carolina for a long weekend getaway. Hilton Head is known for its golf courses and resorts. Since the fall season is a great time of year to play golf, Daddy intended to play a little and I asked to join him.

Daddy tried to teach me how to play golf when I was in high school. I pretended to play, really. I was impatient and stubborn and kept making the same mistakes while we golfed at our county country club. I never listened to his advice. I was truly an embarrassment.

But while in Hilton Head, we went out for some father-daughter time even though he knew what he was getting into. Bless his heart. We headed over to Harbor Town Golf Course to play eighteen holes. Because we were a twosome, the golf pro at the club asked if we would mind joining another twosome, another gentleman and his son, to make a four-some. Golf courses like for you to be grouped in fours as it speeds up the round and those playing behind you don't have to wait so long for a single player or twosome to play through. My father said, "No, we don't mind at all."

We teed off and I think it took me several tries just to hit my ball off the tee. I am sure I annoyed my dad and he probably thought it distracted the other two players. However, the son didn't seem agitated at all. He stayed so concentrated on his game. He was a fantastic player. I've always liked golfers and he was around my age. But this chubby and aloof guy was not all that cute. My dad was more interested in this young man because of his outstanding golf shots. He learned from the father that his son was a senior at the University of Texas and his plan after graduation was to join the pro tour. He certainly was good enough to do so. My father thought, *I am going to remember this young man's name.* This student's name was Ben Crenshaw.

I played golf with *Ben Crenshaw!* This phenomenal golfer later won two major championships: the Masters Tournament in 1984 and 1995, not to mention playing well in tons of other tournaments. He became so well-liked as a pro the television announcers dubbed him Gentle Ben. But the Ben I was playing golf with that day was not the same Ben that later caused girls' hearts to flutter because of his blond Beatle-mop hair and tan good looks. Not this Ben. He reminded me of the Pillsbury Doughboy, that chubby icon of the refrigerated and baking products company. He was as round as Humpty Dumpty and the charm he eventually demonstrated wasn't present that day.

Nevertheless, I claimed to know him. Well, that's what I told people. I left out the sour-doughboy part.

Fast forward five years. I've now become a golf groupie, so during my teaching years when spring break week hit the school system, I persuaded my girlfriends to go with me to Hilton Head's Heritage Golf Classic every year. Who could resist? We had the beach, we got to look at cute golfers—oh, those Wake Forest graduates were the dreamiest—and we were on vacation.

In 1979, my running buddies and I became separated after stalking, uh, following, some of those Wake Forest golfers. I ended up alone near the clubhouse trying to find my fellow educators. Tipsy from beer, I wandered around looking for my friends. There were no iPhones in 1979. We didn't expect to become separated, so there wasn't a game plan. But then I saw a familiar face. As the visage approached, I was excited to see someone I knew! It was Ben Crenshaw and his entourage. Closing in on them, in my confused state, I yelled out, "Hey! Ben!"

He stopped. And his entourage stopped with him.

What had I just done?

I was twenty-five. Lost. Naïve. Brazen. And intoxicated.

And there I was, standing out like a sore thumb in my floral pink golf skirt by Lilly Pulitzer with a white sleeveless but collared Polo shirt. I had on my Kelly-green Pappagallo flats with a brass buckle over the top. Since it was April, I had on a matching green cardigan sweater in case the weather cooled later in the day. My watchband was grosgrain pink and green. I carried my interchangeable-covered Pappagallo Bahama pink purse—monogrammed with my initials, of course, in Kelly-green. My long blonde hair was held back with a pink plaid hair band. I already had a tan from lying out on warm weekends in Atlanta, and wearing all of these colors, I looked like a mixed fruit bowl.

And here I was, face-to-face with Gentle Ben, who by now had dropped that baby fat and was looking mighty good!

I stammered, "I played golf with you here a few years ago."

Ben said, "Oh, yeah? Is that right?"

"Yes, that's right. My dad and I played golf with you and your dad right here on this very course."

Now, for some reason, the TV announcers would get Ben and Tom Kite confused when broadcasting the televised tournaments, but really there was *no* confusion in the way they looked. I think it was because they both played for and graduated from the University of Texas around the same time. Knowing that, he said, "Are you sure it wasn't Tom Kite?"

I thought, you know, he doesn't remember. It was just five years ago. Didn't I disturb his game with my lousy attempts? Wasn't I cute enough for him to *remember me*? I wanted to make sure he knew that I was not talking smack, or worse, flirting with him. I did play golf with him. And to prove it, I needed to mention something that would jog his memory.

So, I said, "No, really. It was you, because you were *fat* then!"

There was mild laughter from the group that followed him and then he quietly and humbly said, "Yeah. I was."

S'il vous plaît excusez-moi

I should be ashamed of myself. I like pulling pranks on people when it looks like I can pull a good one to entertain myself, and others, who will be in on the joke. I know to some it may seem cruel, but I guaran-damn-tee ya that I have set myself up to be made the fool or butt of the gag, and if I can laugh at myself, the victims of my antics should be able to, too.

With that said, I pulled a good one over on a gal who was none worse for the wear. I was playing in a bridge circle which met at members' homes for cards and delectable refreshments. It wasn't a serious bridge club but a social one. I learned to play a bit after retirement. My neighborhood had this card group, and on the last Wednesday of every month, we met at our clubhouse to play and enjoy lunch together. It served two purposes: 1) we supported our clubhouse by having about twelve ladies monthly to buy lunch there, and 2) it was a more social time to catch up with each other.

My mother played in a bridge club. Among her acquisitions I discovered after she passed, was a Goren Point Count Bidding Wheel, which rotated for quick reference on how to help the bidding process in the game. In bridge, so much of it is about the bidding. I took the wheel with me to my group so it would help guide us—especially me—when bidding.

One Wednesday after lunch up at the club, everyone left except four of us who decided we could stay a little longer to play a bit more. Before we began, one of our foursome placed her cell phone down on the bridge table as she excused herself to go to the ladies restroom. The rest of us sat down and started shuffling the cards, waiting for her return, when her phone started ringing. We knew she would show up at any moment, so I answered her phone after seeing on the caller ID that it was one of our bridge club members who had already left. And this is where the fun began.

I said, "*Bonjour!*"

Of course, my greeting startled her.

She responded, "Oh, dear. I am so sorry. Do I have the wrong number? I am trying to reach my friend. I wanted to ask her a quick question about something."

Since our missing card player, who was still in the restroom, would arrive momentarily, I continued my ruse until she did. I started repeating every French rote phrase I learned in ninth grade French class: "*Parlez-vous français?*" Do you speak French? "*Comment allez-vous?*" How are you? "*Mon nom est Lee.*" My name is Lee. I mean, they were all nonsensical ramblings strung together.

She begged, "Oh, please, please excuse me. I thought I was calling my friend. I am so sorry." After her apologies, she hung up.

You know what happened next, don't you? She thought *she* had the wrong number and tried it again. Our friend hadn't returned, so, once more, I answered her phone and repeated, "*Bonjour!*" I echoed everything I had said originally, verbatim, but she still didn't catch on. This is when I realized the caller hadn't taken French lessons, so I decided to add Spanish, "*No comprende*," to the end of my French repertoire. Would she recognize that another language was being spoken? Asking me to once more pardon her, she hung up.

It seems awful that I was having a little fun this way, but I have a *Southern* accent. You'd think it was noticeable that my French wasn't from France. It really sounded more like Pepe le Pew from the *Looney Toons* cartoons. I didn't think it would go this far. And when our friend arrived from the ladies lounge, she saw us all laughing at the fact I had *twice* pulled this practical joke off. We caught her up on the ruse, and when the phone rang for a third time, she answered.

"*Bonjour!*" she reiterated to the caller.

Our sweet friend on the other line was beginning her third round of regrets when she was stopped before she apologized and was told, "You have the right number. We thought for sure you would realize our folly and say something so we could reassure you that we were being absurd." But, bless her heart, she had not. Because she was perplexed the entire time while calling that same number over and over and hearing the French language on the receiving end of her phone call, she thought she had made unnecessary overseas calls.

She then proceeded to call the phone company to tell them her telephone line wires were crossed—wires! this event happened in 2014—and she asked them to please not charge her for those expensive overseas phone calls.

Rain, Rain, Go Away

*W*hile in Raleigh, North Carolina for the wedding and reception of a teacher friend in December 1982, Future Hubby and I met an older gentleman who became interested in our recent engagement and the date we had set for our upcoming nuptials. We replied that we settled on May 14 that coming year.

"May fourteenth, well, well," he said. "According to the *Farmer's Almanac*, the second weekend in May is always the nicest weekend in the South. You should check it out and see for yourself." The next day, we immediately bought a 1983 *Farmer's Almanac* before leaving North Carolina.

Sure enough, the almanac mentioned that the upcoming second weekend in May was the best weekend for farming because of the slightly warmer temps and no rain showers. It was like getting the green light to a perfect wedding day from a crystal ball. We were elated and trusted it completely.

As I counted down the days until the ceremony, I was especially concerned about the weather because my parents and I planned an outdoor reception on my front lawn on the thirty acres where I grew up. Everything for the wedding reception was to be outside—the band, the tables and chairs for guests, the tables for food, the wedding couple's dance, pictures, *everything*.

All this effort made my mother and me especially nervous that the weather might not cooperate. The almanac was the only proven information that it was going to turn out well. But what if there was an off year, and what if it was 1983?

As the wedding day drew closer, my fears heightened, and so did the chance of rain. With only a week to go, the Atlanta news and weather stations reported it did not look all that good. If it rained, how were we going to get all those people in my parents' house? Leaving the church to ride home, getting in and out of the car in my wedding dress, and grey skies in pictures just seemed unthinkable.

In 1983, there were no rental props in my small town. There was no Weather Channel either. I became so concerned that I called the meteorologist at the *national* weather service…every day. I called the national weather office because our local stations didn't see the big weather picture in 1983. They only forecast local weather in the here, now, or tomorrow. I called so much we knew each other on a first name basis. I was totally afraid the weather was going to move in and ruin my day. He assured me that was not going to be the case. All looked clear for that week and weekend from California to Georgia.

Then it happened. There was a squall from the Gulf rumbling into Georgia just two days before the wedding. Mother and I panicked and scrambled to solve the problem. If only we knew someone who had university tailgating tents we could borrow. The only tents we knew about were the tents from our local funeral home…with their name emblazoned across the scalloped hem. They were not even in my wedding ensemble colors. And a few of them might have said, "We're the last to let you down." I was almost in tears.

A day later, the meteorologist and I spoke again and he knew I was in agony. He calmed my fears and told me that there was no need to worry. The storm had moved off in another direction and the next few days were going to be perfect.

And they were.

Note to self: always trust the *Farmer's Almanac*.

"I'm Larry; this is my brother Darrell and my other brother, Darrell."

*D*arrell must not have been a bachelor for very long because after he married, and when his wife became ill for a while, he was in charge of running the house. That's when he got a shock in domesticity. He had to take over all the wifely duties for a short time, and one of those duties was planning and buying the groceries. This was a little tricky for him.

After a few trips, he had an epiphany. He was so proud of this new insight that he shared it with Hubby and me. He said, "Do you know that if you look upwards while in the supermarket, they have *lists* of items that you can find on each aisle?"

Darrell always did and said stuff like that. It wasn't that he was a slow learner, he just didn't pay attention. Let's give the boy some credit—he was a virgin grocery shopper. Naïve. So, hearing about this next encounter from him did not surprise me one bit.

This Alabamian and his wife lived on a large piece of property once owned by his parents. Well thought of, his county's SWAT team asked him if they could use his property for some training maneuvers. He was an easy-going guy and gave them permission. But because he was asked to help them out so far ahead of when the SWAT team needed his property for their practice run, he forgot the date that law enforcement was to appear.

Failing to notice the evening had arrived, he decided to chillax on this summer night even more than usual and went to one of his favorite quiet and secluded spots on his property. He was looking forward to the solitude after his work day. He carried his light-weight portable camp stool with him deep into the woods of his premises. Daddy and I each had an identical stool like Darrell's for our own fishing outings at our pond on our property.

Darrell was all alone in the woods and decided to enhance the relaxing moment by pulling out a joint. This wasn't a usual activity for him, but sitting in a secluded spot and enjoying a toke or two was what he felt he needed at the end of a long and rough day.

Then the unthinkable happened.

Above his head he saw several approaching helicopters flashing huge searchlights around his post. Then a swarm of these Special Weapons and Tactics team members were jumping out of the choppers and crawling all over the place near his isolated location. Running and yelling with arms in hand, they approached closer and closer to Darrell's sanctuary. He froze.

Because of his memory lapse, he rationalized they were coming for him and told us he thought that he better "just kill myself right then and there instead of being caught for smoking pot."

Luckily for all of us, especially for Darrell, he wasn't discovered.

Corndog
Sticks

*I*t started with kindergarten open house. My youngest and I were visiting his classroom and meeting his teacher before the first day of school.

And I was horrified.

She was supposed to be the best teacher in kindergarten. She had been a teacher in the building for several years but in another curriculum. This was her first year teaching five-year-old students and I could tell already we were not going to have a good year.

I taught preschool for my church's kindergarten program. We used these supplies: pencils, crayons, colored pencils, washable markers, regular markers, glue sticks, tape, pencil sharpener, pens, play dough, food coloring, sequins, glitter, stamp pads, sticky Velcro, dry markers—all of which could all be used in science, art, writing, and math-based lessons. Am I right? Of course I am.

So what does one wear to conduct all these tactile lessons? *Not* hose, high heels, and a fancy dress. I don't care if it is an open house. Dress as the teacher you want to personify…someone who came to teach. This was not the evening for parents. This was the children's open house.

I wanted someone who was going to cuddle my snot-nosed child and make him feel good about himself; someone nurturing who might sit on the floor and get dirty with these five-year-olds; someone who knew how to channel boys' frolicsome behaviors; someone who understood squirrelly boys who couldn't sit still. And it wasn't this teacher. I knew just by her appearance she wasn't going to be hands-on.

I am an only daughter, so I can say this: having a female child is way different than boys. I am not saying easier, just different. And her only child was a daughter.

I received notes home about our son's antics almost every day: "Your child stepped on another boy's shoelaces in the hall." "Your child did not come back from the playground after recess fast enough." But the real clincher was, "Your child put his corndog sticks up his nose at lunch." Really?

As a former high school teacher, what if I wrote a note home about some of my students' behaviors?

"Your tenth grader blew his nose too loudly five times during the state assessment exam that we took which might have disturbed the other students and caused concentration problems."

"Your child was flirting with another girl in class when everyone in the school clearly knows that he is going steady with Pat Ann, the most popular girl in eleventh grade and who is a possible future homecoming queen, which would absolutely break her heart if she knew."

"Your eighth child came to school this morning with a suck bump (hickey) on his neck. We just thought you should know."

My own mother, a former teacher for thirty-seven years, commented, "Who has time to write that many notes every day and who is watching those other students when she does?"

I was so pissed at this teacher's bias against boys that at the end of the school year—I didn't want to rock the boat any more than it already was rocking by complaining all year to an administrator—that I bought the book *Bringing Up Boys* by James Dobson, made an appointment with the principal of the school, handed my gift to him, and asked him to place it in the professional library at his school. And by the way, would he please have his teachers read it before next school year? It was too late for us.

And then, as a Mama Bear, I finally wrote back:

Dear Teacher,
You pointed out our son's behavior at lunch. I would like to put things in perspective. At least they were his corndog sticks and his nose.

There were worse things in life.

"Who's Been Sleeping in My Bed?"

or Christmas one year, I ordered and gave myself Ancestry's special offer of a home DNA investigation kit. It really didn't tell me anything I didn't already know—except for my 9% Iberian Peninsula relatives —but just strengthened my genetic history.

While in college, I dated a guy who knew a guy who was on a full basketball scholarship for a large university in the ACC. This athlete had it all—looks, smarts, athleticism, character, manners, and, of course, charm. He wasn't heading to the NBA after college, but no matter, this guy didn't need a pro career in sports. Because of the aforementioned traits, after graduation, he was going places.

He attended law school at New York University to study tax law. Being brilliant and with grades to match, he received a job offer in Boca Raton, Florida. He started working with a firm, but not too long after, set up his own practice and did very well. With all the various businesses in Boca, a tax attorney was invaluable. He married a beautiful and accomplished woman, had five adorable children, lived in a very upscale gated community of million-dollar homes, kept physically active, and yada, yada, yada. You know what I'm talking about. He had it all. Or did he?

He was busy in his charity work and was on several boards to schmooze his practice's profile in his community and state. Oh, he had a big heart. But it didn't hurt to politic in his community. He garnished big-named clients. Money was grand. Life was good. And like Lady Violet Grantham from the television series *Downton Abbey* mentioned, "Nothing says success like excess."

Then a shoe dropped. One day, a neighbor wrote and mailed an anonymous letter to him at his office which informed him that over the course of a few years, she noticed a certain behavior regarding his family and home and felt she should now reveal what it was she'd observed. The letter stated that several days a week, a regular caller frequented his home, arriving after he left in the morning for work and while the children were off at school. This visitor stayed several hours inside their home. The most obvious sign of constant visitation by the same individual was an identical car parked, she supposed without worry of being seen, in the driveway each time. She knew it to be the same car because it was a marked vehicle—the gated neighborhood's security patrol automobile.

Wait a minute. Had she said "years"?

He was a lawyer. He knew what to do. He started collecting evidence. Without his wife's knowledge, he rummaged through his home for clues. It wasn't long before he found a stack of clandestine letters. These letters indicated that his wife and the neighborhood security guard had a past together. They had known each other previously in high school, where, at one time, they had been sweethearts. She a cheerleader and he the hunk football captain—trite, yes—had separated after graduation. The twosome at some point realized they were again thrown into close proximity and picked up where they left off before her marriage to her attorney husband. And adding more salt to the wound, the letters dated back longer than four years! This affair had been going on such a long time, he realized, that two of his five children were born after it began.

He had to find out the truth. Were these last two his?

How he carried on normally without his wife's suspicion was beyond comprehension. But he did. So, while playing it cool, he took the youngest two of all his children to have DNA tests. In the 1990s, this was not done in the comfort of your own home with home kits.

When the results came back, his suspicions proved conclusive—these two youngsters whom he loved with all his heart were not biologically his. He never told his wife about these tests results. He did proceed, however, with a divorce on the grounds of adultery. And while at court to settle the child support requests for five children, he let the other shoe drop. He told her he was not about to pay child support for the youngest two children as the genetic testing proved he was *not* the father.

It was said that her friends and family had to literally carry her out of the courthouse because of her hysterics.

Yes, *Downton Abbey*'s Lady Violet also said, "We all have chapters we'd rather keep unpublished."

It's too late.

Presidential Pets

I always said that I would stay out of the political fray. I am *not* discussing politics in these columns. I refuse to express my opinion about anything to do with our current political situation. But I am going to break that rule here and now. As far as I know, President Trump does not currently have a pet in the White House. And that just ain't right.

From George Washington's American Staghounds, Coonhounds, and Greyhounds, United States presidents and their families have often had pets while serving in office. I especially like knowing about the pets and the names they were/are given and why, if there is a story to be told.

President Theodore Roosevelt had more than dogs while he served in office. His collection included guinea pigs, ponies, a hen, a lizard, Manchester Terrier, a blue Macaw, a garter snake, mixed breed dogs, other terriers, a small bear, a piebald rat, a badger, a regular pig, a rabbit, Mongrel, a Pekingese, a Bull terrier, cats, a hyena, a Saint Bernard, barn owl, a Chesapeake Bay Retriever, and a one-legged rooster. That sounds about right.

Do you know about the rumors surrounding Franklin Roosevelt, who, in 1944, accidentally left behind his Scottish terrier, Fala, in the Aleutian Islands where he visited? *At the taxpayers' expense*, he spent thousands of dollars to retrieve his dog. He explained, "You can criticize me, my wife, and my family, but you can't criticize my little dog." That's good enough for me.

Other presidents who owned and loved their pets include John Adams, Thomas Jefferson, James Madison, James Monroe, John Quincy Adams, Andrew Jackson, Martin Van Buren, William Henry Harrison, John Tyler, James K. Polk, Zachary Taylor, Millard Fillmore, Franklin Pierce, James Buchanan, Abraham Lincoln, Andrew Johnson, Ulysses S. Grant, Rutherford B. Hayes, James A. Garfield, Chester A. Arthur, Grover Cleveland, Benjamin Harrison, William McKinley, William Howard Taft, Woodrow Wilson, Warren G. Harding, Calvin Coolidge, Herbert Hoover, Harry S. Truman, Dwight D. Eisenhower, John F. Kennedy, Lyndon Johnson, Richard Nixon, Gerald Ford, Jimmy Carter, Ronald Reagan, George H.W. Bush, Bill Clinton, George W. Bush, and Barack Obama. How many of you know your presidents? Did I leave out anyone?

I am not saying Trump doesn't have a pet in the White House, we just don't know yet. But I hope he does. And what he might name one would be interesting. One daughter is Tiffany and a son is Barron. Would his pets' names be as interesting? I had a friend who named his Golden Retriever Midas. That might be a name he'd like.

My baby is named after a *Looney Tune* cartoon character —of course. Who didn't love Mel Blanc, the one-man talent behind all the cartoon voices? Although Foghorn J. Leghorn was my favorite, I couldn't help but be impressed with his Southern colonel, all dressed in white like KFC's Colonel Sanders, calling his dog with his syrupy Southern accent from the front porch of his plantation home, "Oh, Belvedere! Come heah, boy!" I introduced the YouTube thirty-second clip to my husband from that scene during our cocktail hour one night and we both cracked up. A couple of dry martinis later, we were crying from laughing so much. Belvedere was out somewhere way, far away on the property. Hearing his master's voice, he came a-runnin'...over bogs, under fallen tree limbs, all the while being distracted by squirrels and rabbits, until after some length of time he finally made his way home. But because his erratic journey took so long, the colonel gave up and went inside before his faithful companion made it to the front door. And, of course, the look on Belvedere's face was priceless: "What the...?"

So, after cocktails, we named our Schnauzer: Oh! Belvedere! or OBie, for short. Remember your *Looney Tunes* days? You might enjoy a step back in time, so head to YouTube for a peek.

I love learning how dogs get their names.

Dag Nab It!

I am totally excited. My favorite historical fiction series, *Outlander*, is starting season three September 10. Are you familiar? *Outlander* is a British-American television drama series based on the historical time travel *Outlander* series of novels by Diana Gabaldon. This author has written eight books in this series and I believe is working on a ninth. Each book is at least eight hundred pages. My book club introduced me to her first book, and when I read the synopsis, I was totally turned off: a married World War II nurse who, in 1945, finds herself transported back to 1743 Scotland, encounters the dashing Highland warrior Jamie Fraser, and becomes embroiled in the Jacobite risings. Time travel? Not a fan of fantasy.

But several years later, I saw the STARZ cable network's first season and was hooked. Time travel only played a minor transportation part to get our nurse from here to there. I mean, Gabaldon didn't go into detail describing it. It was just a means to get her back in time. And when she landed in Scotland, oh, my, I was mesmerized. And then when I saw Jamie Fraser…that's all she wrote.

My maternal grandmother, McCollum, came from a Scotch-Irish heritage. While watching the TV series, the writers had several different Scots say, "Good luck to ya!" in various situations. I heard my mother say that on many occasions. "Mother, I am running to the store to pick up…" "Good luck to ya!" "Mama, I am nervous about my test on…" "Good luck to ya!" No matter how large or small a situation, as I left to act on something, her response was the same, "Good luck to ya!"

It made me think that maybe this was some saying passed down by the Scottish McCollums and without knowing it they might be repeating something from generations ago without thinking…just a rote statement.

Once, while at the nail salon, I heard a thirty-plus-year-old gal who was on the phone and sitting next to me declare, "Dag nab it." After her conversation, I found out her age and then asked her about her saying "dag nab it." If you remember, that expression was repeated on the Appalachian family TV show *The Real McCoys* (1957-1962) by Walter Brennan, as Amos McCoy. He delivered the line, "Dag nab it, Luke!" whenever he was frustrated with his grandson, played by Richard Crenna.

She wasn't old enough to hear it first hand and explained she heard her mother express that saying all the time and picked it up from her. See? She didn't know its origin. It was her mother's habit to use that phrase and now another generation is borrowing it.

Now, what remarks are we Southerners passing down to our children and possibly theirs? Let's take a look at a few:

1. He's a tall drink of iced tea.
2. They're as happy as clams at high tide.
3. They're finer than frogs' hair split four ways.
4. He's as happy as a dead pig in the sunshine.
5. She's got more style than Carter's got liver pills.
6. She's as wild as a June bug on a string.
7. She's madder than a wet hen.
8. He's as crooked as a barrel of snakes.
9. You can't make a silk purse out of a sow's ear.
10. She's as jumpy as a cat on a hot tin roof.

What are we, heah in the South, inherently demonstrating in language to our future children?

If you are unsure of the meaning of some of these Southern cultured similes and metaphors—which is just a drop in the bucket of what's out there—just ask your grandparents, because Mamaw, Big Daddy, and these aphorisms go together like peas and carrots.

Serenity Now

*I*f you are/were a *Seinfeld* junkie like me, you will remember *The Serenity Now* episode. It aired in the U.S. on October 9, 1997. Frank Costanza, Jerry's oldest friend's father, was advised to say, "Serenity now" every time he got angry in order to keep his blood pressure down.

The plot of this episode was inspired by the real-life events of one of the *Seinfeld* writers, Steve Koren. While driving with his arguing parents, Koren was bewildered to hear his father shout, "Serenity now!" at the top of his lungs as part of a rage controlling exercise his doctor had told him about. He then questioned his dad if whether or not the phrase was meant to be yelled as Frank Costanza does on the show.

I need some serenity in my life. For many years, I have sporadically attended yoga, which is a group of physical, mental, and spiritual practices of disciplines that originated in India. It has become popular as a system of physical exercise across the Western world. I'd say it helps.

I now have a waterfall in my sunroom and wind chimes right outside on my deck. I am trying to get there.

I also say the *Serenity Prayer* by Reinhold Niebuhr (1892-1971): "God grant me the serenity

to accept the things I cannot change; courage to change the things I can; and wisdom to know the difference…"

Then there is Karma, derived from India, meaning action, word, or deed, and which also refers to the spiritual principle of cause and effect where intent and actions of an individual (cause) influence the future of the individual (effect). Good intent and good deed contribute to good Karma and future happiness, while bad intent and bad deed contribute to bad Karma and future suffering. Well, it must be real. Karma took a bite out of me.

Once, in the late 1980s, while having an early morning breakfast at McDonald's, I spotted an attractive older gentleman. This refined man with his bald head was with a darling little girl who I supposed to be his granddaughter because of the age difference. Thinking I was complementing him on his descendant, I commented, "What a darling grandchild." He shot back, "Shame on you. This is my daughter." I hadn't expected that. I mean, this was the 1980s. Bald was bald and not a look a man was striving to achieve to be attractive.

Even with those good intentions, Karma came knocking in 1993 to get back at me. I was forty when our second child arrived. My dear, dear friends who knew how long we attempted to have a second child were thrilled for us and gave a baby shower for me which included so many girlfriends from far and wide. I was overwhelmed by the number that arrived and with the outpouring of happiness and love for my family. I brought our two-month-old addition for everyone to see. We already had an eight-year-old son, I had returned to my teaching position, I was exhausted all the time, and I looked it. And I cried a lot. That shower was no exception, as my heart was so full.

Getting low on diapers for the following week, I stopped at the grocery store on my way home. I looked like a hot mess. My makeup had dripped down the front of my face, my eyes were red from the crying jag, and I hadn't slept much the previous night because of dealing with a two-month-old who wasn't sleeping through the night yet.

Checking out, a young man bagged my groceries and then asked if he could assist me to my car as it had started raining.

He had an umbrella and I had a baby and buggy full of groceries. Of course he could help. As he pushed my cart for me while I held the baby and the umbrella for all of us, he said…wait for it,

"Is this your grandbaby?"

Although he never knew why, all I said to him was, "I deserve that."

*H*ere is the entire prayer:

God grant me the serenity
to accept the things I cannot change;
courage to change the things I can;
and wisdom to know the difference.
Living one day at a time;
enjoying one moment at a time;
accepting hardships as the pathway to peace;
taking, as He did, this sinful world
as it is, not as I would have it;
trusting that He will make all things right
if I surrender to His Will;
that I may be reasonably happy in this life
and supremely happy with Him
forever in the next.
Amen.

You've Come a Long Way, Baby!

I've been doling out the advice lately. Today, I am giving you tips on how to better discipline young children. Mine are grown. There is nothing more I can really do except let them figure it out for themselves. You still have another option.

In the early 1990s, I had been out of education for a decade. Did I really want to go back? I tried my hand at substitute teaching first, you know, the job that doesn't have much respect by students. Their mentality was, "How much can we get away with today with this stupid person?" I had four years previously in the classroom and knew what they were thinking, so I decided to beat them at their own game.

Students' parents signed a waiver if an image of their child could be used in any media—school calendars, newspaper stories of school events, and any other kind of video recordings that might be used in the media. But nothing was said of audio recordings. So, every middle or high school I walked in to "babysit," I first stopped by the media center, asked for a tape recorder and blank tape, walked confidently toward the classroom with both, and set the recorder at the front of the classroom for all to see. When the bell rang to start class, before I took roll, I proceeded to tell the reason for the recording device. I was going to record their voices and behavior that day and give it to their teacher along with my notes about this particular class. I would place my notes and the tape in her teacher box to have immediately when she checked for an update of how things went while she was absent.

After that announcement, in front of the entire class, I pushed the record and play buttons simultaneously to start recording. I pushed them with grandeur to dramatize the moment so they were aware that their behavior was being monitored starting at that point. Everything was transparent.

Believe me, it worked. Sometimes, when the class was a little rowdy and I called down a student or two, their voice could be heard on tape first, followed by their name: "Abigail? Settle down a bit." Once, the recorded behavior that I used enhanced a case about a student who was disruptive with his regular teacher.

I tell mothers today about how they can goad their children into line immediately at home or, just as importantly, in public! Wish I could have taken my own advice. My boys are thirty-two and twenty-four. In this eight-year age difference, there were inventions that did improve my mothering capabilities from the oldest to the youngest. But what I needed most hadn't been invented yet—the photo/video options of the cell phone.

Why did I need this phone function and what do I tell mothers today about why they should photograph/video record their own children? Because when children, like my own did at times, start acting out—*record* it. There really is no discussion when you disagree over the behavior you want changed. The child sees his/her action that you want thwarted and instead of intentionally not remembering or really not remembering, the incident is captured to hone in on the behavior you want improved.

Again, you're welcome.

A Brave
New World

*H*ubby and I recently took a little weekend getaway with our oldest son and his girlfriend. They are Millennials. According to the U.S. Census Bureau, this age group numbers 83.1 million, and we went with two of them to Asheville, North Carolina.

We are sixty-four and Baby Boomers. There are generational differences, but I guess you've heard.

The trip was really different. I enjoyed our expedition, but I experienced several firsts (I will put an asterisk beside the firsts).

1. We drove, and Hubby and I took *our* car. It is bigger. The Heir and his girlfriend both drive small Volkswagens. They really don't drive their cars much. Living in Reynoldstown in Atlanta, they catch MARTA to go to work. So, we drove.

2. Another reason we drove is because our oldest wanted to take his Boxer. We *love* our grand-dog and have kept him many, *many* times while our son traveled. Not just short jaunts here or there, but big jaunts—South Africa, New Zealand, Iceland, Europe, Hawaii, and China, to name a few. Millennials like to travel if they can. And when they travel, they stay in hostels, Airbnbs, or outside. Millennials are fond of camping—and so are their pets. So, we took his dog. Because we took his dog, we stayed in an Airbnb*.

We rented an entire house. The description said pet-friendly. The owner even left his cat, Bruce, to hang around. Luckily for the cat, the grand-dog gets along with felines. There was only one bathroom though. I would have picked a place with two. One bathroom didn't seem to matter much to our son, who selected the place. Remember, he loves camping. But there was a fenced-in backyard to let the dog out without supervision at all times. So, as I said, we stayed in a one-bathroom Airbnb whole house for the dog.

The Airbnb house did not have regular TV like you would find in most of our homes. Some Millennials—like our renter, who is one, too—do not even have a TV and will watch media over the internet using smartphone, tablets, or a monitor connected to the internet. Luckily, our son has the same media setup so he knew how to operate the remote. We also used our iPhones a lot. Remember, this group was the first to grow up with computers in their homes and the first generation of kids to grow up with the internet.

> 3. Our entire entertainment involved visiting Asheville's breweries and pubs. Because son and Hubby have a common hobby—brewing their own home-made beer— this was the point, really, of the entire trip. Millennials love their beer. I have become quite fond of the craft beers. But when you've seen one mash tun, you've seen them all and that's how Hubby feels about trips to countries with castles. With outdoor seating, some brew pubs welcome dogs. So, as I said, we went to outdoor breweries for the dog.

Because we were visiting local brew pubs that were in close in proximity, we walked everywhere. The Heir made sure our rental was near the action in downtown Asheville.

We also walked to an outdoor concert sponsored by a brewing company that gives their proceeds to cities to enhance bicycle paths. Millennials appreciate green causes.

5. Our plan was if we were over served, we'd called Uber. We called Uber*.

It was a grand weekend exploring Asheville through our Millennials eyes. It was worth what we shelled out to pay for the trip—oops, did I just say that? Well, The Heir did pay for all the expensive craft beer he wanted us to try. We enjoyed being with him and his girl even if we couldn't discuss politics—Hubby and I had already learned that lesson.

In 2016, the Pew Research Center found that Millennials surpassed Baby Boomers to become the largest living generation in the United States. If by the standards of the U.S. Census Bureau, and based on Pew's definition of the generation, which ranges from 1981 to 1997, we Boomers only total 74.9 million to their 83.1 million.

It's a brave new world.

And don't get me started how Millennials *never answer their phone calls*! They tend to only communicate by texting. No voice interaction. You know what I am talking about.

A Hurricane
by Any Other Name May Not
Sound So Sweet

*W*hat's with the hurricane names like Harvey and Irma? If they were named something more destructive, like Hurricane Death-Megatron-500, everyone would evacuate immediately.

I was in a hurricane in Destin, Florida in 1995. Her name was Erin. In 1950, the formal practice for storm naming was first developed by the U.S. National Hurricane Center for the Atlantic Ocean. Storms were named using the alphabet (i.e., Andy, Bill, Charlie) and these names were the same for each hurricane season. When a new season of hurricanes came around, it was always the exact same names and same order.

To avoid the repetitive use of names, the system was revised in 1953 so that storms would be given female names. The National Weather Service was mimicking the habit of Naval meteorologists, who named storms after women just like ships at seas were traditionally named for women. And to think I thought they were named after women because of this quote I once heard, "I'm not as cooperative as you might want a woman to be." That sounds like a "her"-ricane to me. In 1979, the system was revised again to include both female and male hurricane names.

Our 1995 Erin was pretty tame by comparison to these in the news lately. It was the fifth named tropical cyclone and the second hurricane of the unusually active 1995 Atlantic hurricane season. On July 22, it began as a tropical wave off the coast of Africa and crossed most of the Atlantic Ocean without developing. By July 31, it developed a closed circulation and became Tropical Storm Erin. When it made landfall on the central eastern Florida coastline on August 2, it came in as a Category 1. But moving up to the Florida Panhandle, struck again on August 3 as a Category 2, causing a moderate amount of damage because of its peak strength of 100 mph winds and 973 millibars in central pressure just prior to its second landfall.

We owned a condo in a midrise development. The building was swaying, I suppose to give way instead of break as our sliding glass doors were bowing in. In 1993, we did not have hurricane doors, which we eventually replaced because of Opal two months later. But this storm didn't have much of a surge and therefore didn't cause much damage. As a matter of fact, after it passed, we went outside and took pictures on the beach and Alvin's Alley, a locale at many resort towns, printed T-shirts right off the bat that we wore the next day saying, "I survived Erin."

Our oldest child was ten at the time and he and his cousin were participating in a week-long Marine Biology Camp at the Gulfarium. Erin hit on a Wednesday. They were able to get in their first two days of camp, then the hurricane, and finally the last two days. What was so interesting about the last two days of camp was they saw marine life they hadn't seen in their first two days. I guess we got our money's worth after all.

Although a Category 2, we didn't lose power, but two months later, in rolls Opal, a Category 4. It destroyed our condo. Our condo's roof was made with tar and pebbles and they were blown into our glass sliding glass doors and windows. And then, of course, the rain came in and made a mess. Boardwalks, landscaping, balconies, and railings were destroyed as well. The pool had crazy stuff in it.

After more than thirty years, we sold our second home this year. When hurricane season starts rolling around again, I might be extremely glad we did.

I Am Not
Sweet

My neighborhood has a Sunshine Committee. My school had one, too. The intent of the Sunshine Committee "gifts" is to provide a small token of esteem and consideration when faculty members/neighbors are celebrating a happy occasion or facing a challenging time in their lives. I was once the captain of the neighborhood group. To learn about our residents' concerns, needs, or happy events, I asked for twelve volunteer co-captains of various ages, interests, and different address locations throughout my community so that we might hear about where our committee was most needed in our growing neighborhood.

Another reason for twelve co-captains was to have each lady only being personally responsible for one month of their choosing throughout the year. I just kept the machine running during the year by little reminders about their volunteer commitment. These co-captains, in turn, had a sign-up list of residents who offered their services and were willing to look after any of their nearby homeowners during especially trying times. With the thirteen of us listening out to help others, we covered the 'hood pretty well.

When I signed up to cook an entire meal for someone and dropped it off at the front door, over the years, the home-owner would often tell me, "You are so sweet to do this."

I am not sweet! I may be nice, considerate, kind, friendly, welcoming, courteous, gracious, helpful, or well-mannered— no, I am not that either. I mean, as a Southern Belle, I know better, but I can't help myself sometimes—but I am certainly not *sweet*! And I would say so immediately after I received that compliment, which took the receiver of my kind-heartedness aback. I would say, "I am *not* sweet."

Now, let me tell you what sweet stereotypically is: Someone who is good-natured. They are generally upbeat. They are admired. They are amiable, pleasant, and genial but are often naïve individuals who can be something of a pushover and rarely stands up for oneself. And sometimes icky, sweet people make me sick. Just like real edible sweets, how much can one take and how can someone be *that* good and perfect all the time? *Yuck!*

So, I stop that idea of being sweet in its tracks. Because let me tell you who is sweet: Rose Nyland from the *Golden Girls* TV show. You can't help but love, love, *love* her, but I swear, the rest of her roommates could really run all over her. Am I right? Luckily for her, she didn't always know it, and is that another description of sweet?

I'd rather be nice. I think nice is the same as sweet without the pushover part, or the cheerful-disposition-all-the-time part, or maybe even the stupidly-happy part. I wish I could say the other Betty White performance as Sue Ann Nivens from *The Mary Tyler Moore Show* demonstrated the nice personality. While the character of Sue Ann projected the image of a sweet, perfect wife and homemaker, she was really sardonic, man-obsessed, and competitive, with a tumultuous home life off-screen. Despite her dimpled smile, she could be cruel and snide to people she did not like or considered a threat.

I cannot. But at least they made her *real* for a fictional situation comedy.

As a wordsmith, communication matters. Using the right words matter. Description matters. And I am telling you for the last time, don't ever call me sweet. *I am not sweet.*

Pride Goeth
Before a Fall

*I*t ain't pretty to watch youth turn into old age, is it? On the plus side is the wisdom one gains from life's trials and tribulations. The negative is all that pretty wastes away. And we're all pretty until we're not. I don't mean to sound morbid, I am just trying to be realistic because I sure didn't think it was going to happen to me. No, sir.

I remember visiting the ladies restroom in downtown Atlanta's Rich's Department Store when I was about ten years old. Never had I seen so many women in sleeveless dresses with droopy upper arms. How embarrassing for them! I remember thinking to myself, "When I get old, that's not going to happen to me. No, sir."

In my thirties and never having worn glasses, I was selling real estate for a regional developer. I wanted to appear older and wiser than my years suggested, so I made an appointment with my friendly ophthalmologist. He gave me non-prescription glasses, no cheap grocery store brand, to wear to make me look smart. How dumb was that? I thought I'd never have to wear real prescriptions with my 20/20 vision. No, sir.

Then my forties appeared. Guess what? It was the beginning of the end, and it was…glasses. I succumbed and bought my first pair at the pharmacy. I started with the lowest level, but I didn't stay there. Reading glasses and I have a long history. Yes, sir.

Here came the fifties. In the early part of that decade, while eating deviled crab at a local restaurant and taking that first scrumptious bite, part of a broken crab shell was in my forkful. I felt a crack to a back molar and a horrific shooting pain through my nerve. One of my few fillings came in contact with agony which seared through my right molar's nerve. A year and a half later, the left mirror image molar cracked and broke. I had lived until almost sixty years and had never seriously fractured any part of my body until now. And here I was dealing with my first major dental catastrophe and the expensive fallout—years of dealing with two no-insurance-coverage dental implants. Yes, sir.

I remember reading Nora Ephron's *I Feel Bad About My Neck* while still in my fifties, and thought, *What the heck is she talking about? Neck?* I wasn't paying attention to necks because I remembered Rich's and those bird-flapping-arm women. Neither had happened. But then—you guessed it. Here came that neck, and a few years later, the arms, too. Yes, sir.

I was falling apart. I had nothing left to be proud of. Oh, wait. I remember getting compliments on my feet. People would tell me how patrician and pretty they were. And I'd show them off wearing the prettiest of toenail polish and open-toed shoes, sandals, or flip flops. My pride and joy. I saw myself in my sixties not looking like the girl of my youth. But my feet! Those toes! I still had those! I would lie in bed and raise my legs to enjoy my pretty, slim, compli-mented feet because that's all I had left!

And then God gave me a wake-up call. One day while in a hurry, I clumsily ran into my laundry room door and broke my second and longest toe. And there it went...my last hold-out of anything pretty left on this ole body of mine. Yes, sir.

Boo!

My neighborhood plays the game, You've Been BOOed. Some might call it Ghosting or The Phantom. It's a friendly, innocent prank for Halloween fun. We have a lot of children in our neighborhood, so the game starts early in October.

Someone clandestinely starts the game—I know who—by secretly leaving a small Halloween-themed gift bag of treats—and maybe some tricks!—for each child in the selected home. It also contains instructions for the partaking of the fun, a "You've Been BOOed" sign, and a "BOO" poem. After a household has been BOOed, they, too, must in turn secretly pay it forward. Those participating will know when a house has already been BOOed because the sign in the goody bag will be placed on the front door allowing others to move on to another neighbor.

Part of the fun is *how* the rewards are delivered to the chosen homeowner. This is where the covert shenanigans come into play. You must drop off the loot, ring the doorbell, and scamper away before being caught. The children have so much fun with this part.

Day by day, BOO signs proliferate, and soon, the entire neighborhood's front doors are sporting "You've Been BOOed" evidence that indicates someone mysteriously visited them before Halloween night.

Here's what the sign says:

You've Been BOOed

The air is cool, the season fall,
Soon Halloween will come to all.
With ghosts and goblins, and spooks galore,
Trick-or-Treaters at the door.

The spooks are after things to do,
In fact, a spook brought this to you!
The treats that come with this short note,
As yours to keep. Enjoy them both.

Excitement grows when friends like you,
Decide to share this little BOO,
Neighbors will have smiling faces,
None can guess who's BOOed which places.

A day or two to work your spell,
But keep it hidden! Hide it well!
Join the fun, the season's here,
So, spread these BOOs – and share the cheer!

*S*hare the *cheer*? Wait a minute.
   Why should the kids have all the fun? Let the

grown-ups in on it, too. Except, this time, as we share the cheer, the adult version is called, "You've Been BOOzed!"

You've Been BOOzed!

by Guess Who?

It is now October,
There's something's in the air,
But it's just for adults,
So all the rest beware.

This special Halloween
Is different don't you see?
Isn't just for children,
It's just for you and me!

There's someone you may know –
A (name your subdivision here) neighbor –
Who's brought you some bubbly,
I bet you will savor.

When it is all consumed,
It may give the right kick,
You might find there's a treat,
Or might find there's a trick.

Yes, now it is your turn,
To pass along delights,
For someone else to sip…
Before Halloween Night!

*Y*ou have my permission to borrow.
Happy Halloween!

Name Calling

*D*id you have a hard time naming your children? When I hear from teachers, they especially find it hard to name one of their own after teaching a few rascals so that they wouldn't *dare* use the names of those students for their own. They might turn out like those little hooligans!

I enjoyed the book *Freakanomics* by Steven D. Levitt and Stephen J. Dubner. The subtitle is *A Rogue Economist Explores the Hidden Side of Everything*. It redefines the way we look at the modern world.

Chapter Six's title is *Perfect Parenting, Part II; or: Would a Rhoshanda by Any Other Name Smell as Sweet?* The topic is that "the belief in parental power is manifest in the first official act a parent commits: giving the baby a name. As any modern parent knows, the baby-naming industry is booming, as evidenced by a proliferation of books, websites, and baby-name consultants. Many parents seem to believe that a child cannot prosper unless it is hitched to the right name; names are seen to carry great aesthetic or even predictive powers."

Is naming destiny?

With our first born, we had a heck of a time. I found the book *Parents Book of Baby Names* by Martin Kelly. It contained the origins and history, their meaning, the nicknames, and derivations of hundreds of female and male names. But then *Freakanomics* made me think—can a name be damaging to one's psyche?

I asked my friends on Facebook to tell me about actual people they know/knew that I could add to the list. These are real people, folks. Remember that while reading. Here they are:

Crystal Fountain was a school mate.

Miss White married Mr. Green and moved to Gray, Georgia.

Another White gal, Bonnie, married Ken Knight. Did you figure out she was then Bonnie White Knight?

Dr. Strait was a Cartersville, Georgia orthodontist.

Jimmy Shivers's father was in the refrigeration business.

A friend's parents' actual names are Dick and Jane.

Someone knows a Jay Bird.

Sonny, Dusty, Wendy, Stormy, and Misty Williams.

A friend worked with a girl named Holly Bush.

Jazzercise instructor had an aunt named Kat Knapp and her daughter-in-law was Nita Knapp.

A neighbor knew a girl in high school named Polly Sachs —pronounced Socks. Her middle name was Esther. Now say it all together…that's right, polyester socks!

I went to college with a Twinkle Starr. Twinkle was born April 1.

A preschool teacher said she went to school with a guy named Rusty Carr.

A high school teacher graduated with a Honey Buns.

Flight attendant knows a Lulu Bob from Tyty, Georgia.

An octogenarian in the neighborhood went to school with Ima June Bugg.

A former choir member of mine knew a Safety Furst and he was a doctor in Oklahoma.

High school girlfriend knew a Brick Stone.

And here's a grand finale name:

A good friend mentioned to me about their friend, Bubba. You know, Bubba is a great Southern name. It usually comes from someone younger in a family calling a male sibling, a brother, Bubba because they can't say brother. And so it sticks. If you live in the South, you know *lots* of Bubbas. But these brothers grow up. Johnny turns into John. Ricky turns into Rick. Billy turns into Bill. But what do Bubbas do? This Bubba turned into a Delta airline captain. He realized how unprofessional it would be if he kept his common name as they announced over the speaker to the passengers, "Ladies and gentlemen, today you will be in the good hands of Captain Bubba."

Live and Learn

*O*h, the trials and tribulations of cooking.

I am in my seventh decade and just found the secret to crisping the perfect bacon…last week. My husband even cooked it better than I ever did. I guess I wasn't paying attention to Mama in the kitchen when she was frying some for breakfast, but now, finally, I have a method that works for me.

Teri Hatcher, the actress from the television shows *Lois and Clark: The New Adventures of Superman* and *Desperate Housewives*, once said in her book, "[Women will say] '… You take the good piece and I'll just take what's left.'" In fact, the title of her new book, *Burnt Toast: And Other Philosophies of Life*, is a metaphor for women who too often take the burnt or the leftovers for themselves.

But in my case, not to be wasteful, somebody had to eat burnt food or my other missteps.

My mother was a fantastic cook, and I bet several of you could say the same about your mothers. But I never watched her magic in the kitchen. The only cooking I did was to read the directions off a Chef Boyardee pizza box in the 1960s. Instructions on the Chef Boyardee Pizza Kit said, "Gives you a chance to make your own homemade 12-inch pizza just the way you like it." It's not really all that hard to make a home-made pizza, but fifty years ago, we also had to make our own dough. Here were the dough directions:

Spray the cookie sheet or round pizza pan with a nonstick cooking spray. Pour the dry dough mix in a bowl. Add 2/3 cups of warm water.

Now, that was the easy party. You had to knead the dough and then try to spread it out across the pre-sprayed pizza pain. Gooey! Sticky! In my case, the dough never stretched all the way to the end of the pan. I tried different shapes: round, square, and rectangle. It never rolled out far enough even with a bit more flour sprinkled on the dough and pushing it to the sides of the pizza pan, which caused holes in your dough no matter how careful you were. It kept sticking to your fingers during this exercise. What took thirty minutes should have taken five.

The rest was easy. It tasted nasty but we didn't know any better.

When I lived in my first apartment in Atlanta, I was having guests for dinner and wanted to do something fancy impressing my guests. I was twenty-two years old and following a marinated chicken recipe to serve my company. I was keeping it simple as a beginner cook since it was my first real foray. Reading the directions from a cookbook, a Christmas gift from mother, it was the most elementary recipe. I don't remember everything it said, but I do remember it called for the old 1970s standby—Italian dressing. After reading the instructions to marinate the meat overnight, I did just that...*on the counter*. It never said to marinate it in the refrigerator! I don't remember anything after that but crying and calling my mother, who suggested I throw it out, of course.

I do remember asking her once early on, "How can you just pull a meal together like you do without a recipe?"

She answered, "When you've done it as long as I have, you just don't need instructions any longer."

But I am becoming absent-minded and wonder if I should write this bacon strategy down, because isn't that life for you: once you learn to master something, then comes the age where you forget what you did.

Gumption

The back book cover and Amazon's description of my teacher book, *She's a Keeper! Cracked Compositions from a Southern Girl's Classroom*, reads: "Lee St. John is a rogue Southern Belle, a high-jinx expert, and mayhem confessor. You will see. Twisted, uproarious, revealing, delicious, quirky, surprising, warm, humorous, heartfelt, or scandalous. Take your pick. You will find them all in these true stories about family, friends, co-workers, and others whose names she cloaks when telling her tales. Well, she had to."

Of course, I had to, but they are the only things that aren't real. Even I operate in disguise. Lee St. John is my nom de plume. I am a maverick, which, by definition, means: an unorthodox or independent-minded person. Synonyms: individualist, nonconformist, free spirit, original, eccentric. I'll take any of those.

My high school conduct grades support this notion. When my husband married me, he stated that he wanted a challenge. Well, he sure got one. Bless his heart. Rules don't apply to me. Where other teachers hung a behavior chart on their classroom wall with line-item rules, my chart just said, "Behave." When a fourth grade teacher once told me to put my second child on a behavior chart at home, I stated, "I can't."

"What do you mean you can't?" she asked.

"Well, I tried to do a chart with my first son. It just didn't work. Not so much for him, but for me. I tried to follow through doing things on a set schedule. I really tried. I had stickers for accomplishments, rewarded him with activities or special food, but I personally just couldn't do it. And my way of thinking is what kind of example am I setting if my children saw that I had set goals of some kind and couldn't carry them through? I thought that display would be worse. 'Do as I say, not as I do'? What kind of precedent would I be setting?"

I only behaved for my parents out of shame. My mother knew how to work me, and I've said many times she should have been a travel agent for guilt trips.

I like mavericks. One of my favorite authors was one. This winner of the Pulitzer Prize for Fiction was as unorthodox as they came in the 1920s. She was an average college student and did not excel in any of the area academics. She was a working woman at a time when women didn't work that much and decided to pursue a career in journalism. She began writing feature articles for *The Atlanta Journal-Constitution*, where she received almost no encouragement from her family or "society."

She was flamboyant, wild, and unrestrained, but because of her family's standing in Atlanta, she was asked to join the Atlanta Junior League. For her debut at the Georgian Terrace Hotel, she prepared a dance with the help of a friend from Georgia Tech. The dance was called the Apache, which was a provocative Parisian street dance of the Jazz Age.

It was a sensational—from what I read, *sin*sational for her day—performance, and afterwards, she was denied membership.

She collected erotic Parisian postcards. She smoked. She drank. She married. She divorced. She remarried.

And she authored *Gone with the Wind*, which was the top American fiction bestseller in 1936 and 1937. As of 2014, a

Harris Poll found it to be the second favorite book of SHE'S A KEEPER! Funny Essays about What *Really* Happens in Teachers' Classrooms. More than thirty million copies have been printed worldwide.

Margaret Mitchell again displayed her non-conformist side when, decades later, the Atlanta Junior League hosted the jubilant citywide premiere party for the film *Gone with the Wind*. Everyone who was anyone associated with the film would be there. Gable, Howard, Leigh, de Havilland, Selznick, and their just as popular dates or spouses. Stubborn, gutsy, and defiant, she *declined* their invitation.

Maverick Margaret Mitchell. Maverick Lee St. John. I'm comfortable with that.

Jive Talking

It was 1993. Scrabble Night. Another couple, Hubby, and I played Scrabble at their home. We brought over our board game from home, kept now in our lake house upstairs closet. It was late and we were almost done. With only four letters left, I played on a triple word score square the word jive. I also used all my letters, which gave me extra points. My husband and I seemingly won the game with that last move.

But our male host was going to have none of it. He said, "There is no such word as jive." His wife begged to differ. She agreed with us that there was such a word. But he was going to have none of it and called it an evening. She was upset with her husband's actions, but we weren't surprised. We had known him for a long time and he thought he was always right. We always just sort of indulged him, but this evening was over. It hadn't come to a natural conclusion, but an abrupt one with his guests beating him in Scrabble, in his own home, and he didn't like that one bit. Nothing more could be said to change his mind, and so, we left.

Taking the Scrabble game home with me, I looked over the rules while Hubby drove—if the word could be found in the dictionary, it was a word. This was way before iPhones and being able to research the word right then and there, so when we made it home, I looked up jive in our dictionary, and there it was. Even though it was very late, I called the host and told him the word was in our dictionary. Within a few minutes, he called back and read the rule that said, "If a word cannot be found in the host's dictionary, it is not a word." He said he could not find the word in his dictionary.

Good grief! How much longer was this going to go on? He was serious. Being a very smart man who won a lot of arguments, and seeing behavior like this before from him, I was at my breaking point. I had enough. I wasn't about to take this one lying down, so I decided I'd try to goad him a little more. I hatched a plan.

This Scrabble playing couple was in our dinner club of five couples. It was time for another dinner club. Ironically, it was to be held at the Scrabble couple's home. Not that it mattered where the dinner club was, but it seemed poetic justice in some ways after I put my plan to work. Karma was about to raise its head.

I called the other three couples, not the entertaining couple—it was going to be a surprise for the host—and begged them to please incorporate the word jive into their conversations throughout the night. For instance, "We went to see a jive of a movie last week." "That's a jive blouse you are wearing." One couple in our group was our church's associate pastor and his wife, and I asked him, while he gave the blessing before our food, to please say something like, "Bless this jiving food."

He did.

All the couples played along during the evening, "jiving" this and "jiving" that in normal conversation. I watched and waited all night to see if he was going to catch what was taking place around him. And finally, when it happened so much and that light-bulb moment materialized, one could see he realized he had been had because his face contorted and he turned and looked over at me and said, "You win."

Happy dance!

I really don't see how some people can *be so stubborn*!

I Feel Bad
About My Neck, Too

*O*kay, girlfriends—let's get real.

If you are over fifty and haven't read Nora Ephron's book, *I Feel Bad About My Neck*, you should. Thank goodness someone is writing about one of the many things that are bothering some of us girls of a certain age.

Let me start off by saying, first of all, after forty, I started needing reading glasses. I guess that's about right. That's about middle ground, maybe forty, plus more good years. My first magnification was .75 on the scale. But now, over the last twenty plus years, that number has risen. I don't know how high the vision number goes; I've seen the number four, but I think I am in the threes.

Then it was the aches and pain commercials. I can remember in my forties s a commercial for a product that promised to reduce muscle aches. A woman that looked just a little older than me was hiking, and afterward, she commented on her muscle ache and recommended Advil, or was it Aleve? I don't remember that part because I was so shocked at someone of "our" age needing something for her pain. I remember thinking, *What is she talking about? That's used for headaches.* Then it happened. Shortly after turning fifty, I was taking something, too. I thought, *Oh, now I get it!*

Next came the neck. I read Ephron's book about ten years ago for the first time because her author picture caught my attention on the back jacket sleeve. She has a turtleneck sweater pulled up and over her chin, obviously hiding her neck. I didn't get that either. Neck? What was she talking about? She was too young to have a neck that bothered her. I mean, that's for old people. She was twelve years older than me and I was in my early fifties, so she was still young. And then, within a couple of years, mine dropped.

And it wasn't pretty.

Being a little plump, mine was what I considered the first of two kinds of necks: a pig neck or a chicken neck. It doesn't matter which one you have, because neither looks good. You can't win for losing. Chicken neck people are usually thin people who look great in clothes but because they are so thin, when they get older, you see every crease and crevice in their skin and especially their neck. It looks like ties on a railroad track.

Then you have the pig neck people. These are the ones with extra weight where the weight settles in the neck. I try to hide my neck. My favorite pose is placing my hand, or hands, under my chin as though I am pondering something. Pig neck people really can't hide their neck because the fat spreads out into the jowls and up towards the ear.

There are pros and cons to being either a chicken neck person or a pig neck person. The cons are they are both ugly, but whereas the chicken neck girl is thin and, on the whole, looks great in clothes, the pig neck person might have prettier and softer skin because there are not many wrinkles in the face because of all the collagen.

I have lost some weight lately and now I am seeing more chicken neck and I am not prepared! I didn't know to put on all the wrinkle creams at bedtime for forty years. I thought I was always going to have collagen!

It's a lose-lose situation. Tell me I'm not right.

Next time, let's talk extra skin arm flapping, which we thought we'd never have either.

It's a Wonder
the Relationship
Lasted This Long

I was once a purse girl, and I've had my share of fashionable ones. But today? Nah.

In the 1960s, I had to have everything John Romain. His fashion was all the rage. In the fall/winter, I carried a leather-handled and wool tweed mid-sized handbag with brass and metal studs and three interior compartments. In the summer, I carried his Wicker Creel Purse. It really looked like a bait basket. Today, several of these vintage handbags are offered on eBay, and the description reads, "...and very clean on the inside!!!!" Four—count 'em, *four*—exclamation points.

Then, in the 1970s, it was everything Pappagallo. The Bermuda Bag was a hit because it was button covered with interchangeable covers. The handles were tortoise shell and covers ranged in design from Scottish tartan for fall/winter change-out, frogs on lily pads for Spring, and watermelon pink with Kelly green piping (or vice versa) or madras plaid for summer. I shopped at the Pappagallo store on Peachtree Road habitually! Now, when these used purses are sold various sites, the copy always mentions, "clean inside."

By the 1980s, I was earthy and carried a Kilim designed pocketbook. It was a beautiful and unique bag made by the Iranian carpet company Matt Camron. It had a drawstring and was fully lined. eBay's ad repeats, "clean."

When the 1990s came along, I was back in traditional mode again and was proud of my Coach purse. No knock-off for me! I had a friend who was the rep for the company. Etsy has one just like mine and describes it this way, "Vintage Coach Willis Bag, British Tan Leather, Satchel Purse, Brief-case Style, Top Handle, Long Adjustable Strap, 1990s. Clean inside."

The 2000s came along, and by this time, I was considering why I wasn't much in a pocketbook mood any longer and bought a Vera Bradley knock-off. It served its purpose, but I was looking to break up this relationship.

By the 2010s, I used the Wonder-Bra-Purse. I called it by that name because all I needed was my bra for the little storage to house the things I needed to take with me while out and about. My car held the rest. I drove to my location, stepped out of my car, completed my mission, stepped back in, and eventually drove home. My car had a visor mirror, a closed compartment behind the gear shift to keep things in like my makeup, a place that kept my brush and my rollers if I decided to take them out of my hair at the last minute—yes, I know better, but still I drove to my location with rollers in my hair—a little square compartment for change that I used for lipstick, and *two* cup holders, where one held coupons, nail file, quarters, and even a Splenda packet for any non-sweetened drink I might purchase when I drove-thru for a fast food order. Tissues went in glove compartment. I mean, who needs a purse?

Oh, the best part…I kept my identification/charge cards—I only charge—in a money clip nestled in my bra. Car keys? Same place, other side. Phone? I carry. I don't want a purse for these reasons:

1. The bottom is *always* a dirty mess whether it's my purse or someone else's. Eww! Partially wrapped gum, pennies, grit, wadded coupons, a french fry

or two, and such can be found, and it gives me the creeps just thinking about it.

2. I learned having a purse when shopping is inconvenient. What do you do with it while rummaging through clothes on a rack or display table? While your regular purse is on your arm with a strap, it's in your way and you have to sling it away from you a million times, or if you leave it in your buggy, it might be stolen should you become distracted or walk away for just a moment.

I'm telling you, the Wonder-Bra-Purse *is* a *wonder*. Just don't be on the receiving end watching me whip out my bank card for you to hold to charge my purchases. Let me do that.

To make you feel more comfortable about my newfangled carryall pouch, the Wonder-Bra-Purse has a pocket behind each cup and, in reality, the charge card never touches skin. TMI? Just thought you should know.

The Customer is Always Right

*L*unching with an Atlanta girlfriend on a Friday, I was asked, "What would you like to drink?"

"A Bloody Mary, please."

"I'm sorry, we don't serve Bloody Marys Monday through Friday. We only offer it on the weekend," the restaurant's hostess answered.

"Excuse me?"

"We have stopped offering Bloody Marys during the week."

"Wait a minute, you mean to say that I cannot order a drink today, Friday, that you serve at this restaurant on the weekends?" I asked.

"That's correct," she said.

"I can order vodka?" I inquired.

"Yes."

"And tomato juice?"

"Yes."

"Can you add that other stuff and not call it a Bloody Mary?" I continued.

"No. We cannot. We only offer our signature Bloody Mary on weekends."

"But you have lemon juice, horseradish, Worcestershire sauce, Tabasco, salt, and pepper?"

"Of course."

"But you can't throw them in with the vodka and tomato juice?"

"We cannot."

"Would you bring them to me and let me mix it up?"

"No."

"Listen, I know you don't want people saying they bought an ordinary Bloody Mary here when you are so proud of your signature drink that you are making it available only on weekends, but I promise I won't diss it. I don't even know what your specialty drink's name is. I just remember getting a pretty good Bloody here for thirty years."

"Management won't let us sell it except on weekends."

"May I see your manager?"

Manager makes himself available and will not budge.

I was in shock that they would refuse my money, for one, and two, not try to please a—future—customer. And I am not alone.

When I returned home, I got online and discovered this:

Reviewed March 4, 2017 via mobile
Bloody Mary Lovers Rejected!

Very strange... [a very popular Atlanta restaurant] has long been a favorite lunch spot. The food is good, not great, but with larger servings than expected. It was also a place to enjoy a good but not great Bloody Mary. When I asked for one last Thursday, I was told "we no longer sell Bloody Marys on weekdays." I laughed, thinking she was toying with me, but, no, she said they had been instructed by headquarters to stop weekday sales as of 10 days ago. She said, since they customize their Bloody Mary mix, too much was being wasted on week days, so, no, I can't have one. I suggested I buy a glass of tomato juice, a shot of vodka and she give me access to other ingredients. That way I make my own. No again, with a laugh. So I asked to speak to the manager. A nice guy came from the kitchen, powerless, saying the bosses have spoken. I have to do what they say.

I suggest he tell their bosses to retake Restaurant Management 101 and note the section on providing customers the products they seek. Liquor service is the profit backbone of most restaurants, with huge profit margins. To refuse to make weekday bloodies is a collective slap in the face to those who, like me, enjoy them, not just on weekends.

We Bloody Mary lovers, and there are many, SHOULD NOT PATRONIZE [restaurant name] UNTIL MANAGE-MENT BRINGS BACK OUR BLOODIES!

PS: MY fish sandwich was good, not great, and at $18.00, overpriced. My 3 stars are for decent food.

*S*ound familiar? Identical experience! And guess what I had ordered for lunch? The fish sandwich. And a beer.

P.S. I found their special drink recipe. Who'd like it?

How Do You Spell F***?

The Spare finished his studies for the day and was playing outside one sunny afternoon. While preparing dinner in the kitchen, I heard the back door slam and feet scamper upstairs. A short while later, there was a knock at the front door. When I answered it, there stood a man in overalls who looked eerily familiar. But since everyone looks like somebody else to me, I quickly figured that this man was the doppelganger of William Frawley. Frawley was a stage entertainer and television actor best known for playing Fred Mertz, the landlord and neighbor of Lucy and Ricky Ricardo, on *I Love Lucy*. He was also Bub O'Casey in the television comedy series *My Three Sons*.

"May I help you?" I asked when I came to my senses after staring for a bit.

He inquired, "Ma'am, do you have any children?"

"I have a son in high school at football practice and an eight-year-old who is upstairs."

"I am sorry to bother you, but do you know if your youngest son has been painting anything today?"

Now he had my attention. Opening the door wider, I said, "He has been outside playing while I was in the kitchen cooking, but I cannot tell you if he has been in paint," hoping he hadn't.

"Well, ma'am, I am the yard man for the house next door. It's for sale, and as you may or may not know, its owners have moved out of state. I have been employed by the real estate office to continue to care for the yard so that the grass doesn't get too high. The real estate office wants it to have a nice curb appeal. While cutting grass in the backyard, I noticed something interesting painted on the crawl space door. Care to take a look with me?"

Uh-oh.

I called to The Spare to come downstairs. He burst down the steps and into the foyer. Then the three of us went over to the neighbor's backyard. This really wasn't a convenient time for me to find out the kind of possible "trouble" my youngest might have met because I left a pot of green beans simmering on the stove—in fatback, I might add, just like my mother used to do—and I was still wearing my mother's hand-me-down apron. It reminded me of her and her delicious cooking when she wore it while I was a little girl. It was a cream-colored Calico cotton all-day bib apron with red piping. Having no-ties, or crisscrossing in the back, it was easy to slip on and off. The light-weight fabric featured barn yard animals on a farm—chickens pecking corn, a red barn, ducks waddling near a stream, and cows in a background pasture. With its two double sewn side pockets, it was a no-brainer to keeps spills and splatters off one's clothing while cooking.

As the three of us walked up to the white crawl space door of the neighbor's empty house, I saw the word "f***" painted in all capital blue letters. My eyes widened. I was horrified. Mortified! Mystified! The man saw my expression and chuckled.

I wondered and asked, "Why did you come to *my* house to ask if this was painted by *my* child?"

The yardman answered, "I followed the paint spills on the grass and they led me to your back door."

I then said it couldn't possibly be The Spare who had done this. The man belly laughed and said he wasn't judging. He had boys of his own who fell into mischief occasionally.

"No, no, you don't understand," I continued. "It's just that I don't think my son could have done this. I mean, it's not that I don't think him *incapable* of painting that word on the crawl space, but because I have been helping him study for his spelling tests at school, it's just that I am shocked he spelled f*** correctly."

One Tomato,
Two Tomato,
Three Tomato, More!

I. Am. In. Heaven. It's fresh tomato season and I made my first purchase at my town square a week ago. *And* my tomato purchases will continue until the last day of anyone's garden producing a home-grown tomato they are willing to sell.

My parents were the best when producing fresh produce. We lived on thirty acres and did not have a fence surrounding our garden. I did not know about and never remembered them bemoaning that deer or other vegetable eating critters ruined all their hard work. My father's name was Darden, and they called their creation Darden's Garden. We had lots of other yields from it: corn, okra, spring onions, butter peas, marigolds, and more.

I remembered picking and shelling peas with my mother. My aunt came over to help and then received her gifts from the garden as a thank you for her help. Although she used glass sterilized Bell jars, Mother, my aunt, and I went to the cannery that our county made available for those who canned their own vegetables. Later, Mother sterilized those jars in our house herself and sealed the goodies. Jars and jars of butterbeans, corn, onions, tomatoes, and okra cooked down in their own juices could be found in her kitchen cabinets just waiting for winter to arrive when potatoes would be added for vegetable soup. Don't forget the cornbread!

I couldn't be the farmer my parents were, but I did try my

hand with my first backyard garden on my 1.3-acre plot where we purchased a home. I planted tomatoes and put up a fence around them to keep out our deer, but I guess it wasn't high enough as our visitors would stick their heads over and would nibble at their early morning breakfast. The next year, I put up a higher fence and moved the produce further away from the fence since they preferred what I valued. That worked better. But trying to weed around the harvest in that chicken wire fence proved difficult.

Then I scaled back and only planted my tomatoes—Big Boys variety!—in containers on my deck. That worked pretty well, and I even felt smug when a girlfriend wrote on Facebook about her disgust of deer somehow getting into her tomato plants even with all the armor surrounding her vegetable garden. I laughed and laughed that day she posted that fiasco, thinking, *That won't happen to me. I am smart. No deer is going to climb up my steps to my deck and eat my tomatoes. Ha-ha-ha!*

The next morning, I woke up to find that I didn't have to worry about the deer eating my plants but something with big teeth shaped like rabbits' choppers had taken just *one* bite out of every single one of my tomatoes. Since it wasn't rabbits hopping up those twenty-plus steps, I didn't know what in the world climbed up my stairs to reach the top deck where my planters were. Somebody tell me! Raccoon? Whatever it was it—they—ruined every ripe one that I was giving *one more day* until perfection with those teeth marks.

"Best laid plans of mice and men."

I got out of the tomato business and left it to the professionals. Although it would be nice to watch tomatoes sprout up on a daily basis, I just didn't want to give those visiting my deck the privilege of snacks. Forage on your own. I feed birds in the winter, but I didn't need a new pet taking the most precious of precious tomatoes from me.

So, with my cherished purchase from Wednesday's downtown Farmer's Market, I had my first tomato. Should I eat it in a sandwich? Nope. Not the first bite of the season—just a little salt, pepper, and mayo. And so it begins for a couple of months. Summer is here!

Next time, we'll discuss which mayonnaise to add. Besides the goodness of the fresh tomato, it's all about the mayo, too, right?

Lewis Grizzard

~ if at first you don't succeed,
try, try, try again ~

*L*ewis Grizzard was one of my favorite writers. When I first taught high school in the late 1970s, I read his *Atlanta Journal-Constitution* columns aloud every morning to my students before I started teaching my English classes. Somewhere I read that if you started the day off with humor, you would get your brain flowing.

He was married four times. Something he said around wife number two, or maybe number three, stuck with me. "We've been married for six weeks and they said it wouldn't last." It was about week six into my marriage that I felt like leaving my husband.

Hubby and I, like my parents, married at thirty. We immensely enjoyed our twenties and felt like when we settled down into a marriage, we would have gotten all the playing out of us. What we didn't know was that we were already set in our ways.

What I loved about my husband was that he wasn't like my father. Now, don't get me wrong, I *loved* my dad, who had many wonderful traits, but my mother babied my daddy because I hadn't been born yet so he was all she devotedly took care of for ten years! I wasn't going to baby my husband…or so I thought. And what he told me about himself while we were dating, I thought would last. I happily discovered that he did his own laundry! He ironed his own clothes! He cooked a bit! He cleaned his own house! *Loved it!*

When I was first invited to have dinner at his home, I

realized all this was true. And that evening, he cooked—okay, they were steaks on the grill, but still, he cooked. He prepared a salad—and this was before salads in a bag so he had to go to some trouble. He added baked potatoes to the equation—yes, he did cook them in the microwave. And get this—he cleared the table, cleaned the dishes, and placed them in the dishwasher. These were his selling points. This was the guy for me!

Then we married.

After the honeymoon, I returned to work and came home those first two weeks tired but happy. We both cooked our meal together, and when we finished dinner, he brought all the dishes to the kitchen and put them in the sink. Two weeks later, he stayed in the kitchen talking to me while I did all the preparation for our dinner, and after our meal, he placed all the dirty dishes on the counter. Then another two weeks passed and I caught him reading the newspaper in the living room while I solitarily cooked our meal, and when he was finished, I noticed he had just left his dirty dishes on the table. I was livid!

I dissected this and realized that I was no June Cleaver from the 1950s television show *Leave It to Beaver*. I was exhausted, and if he thought I was just going to cater to him, he had another think coming.

I was so upset after these first six weeks of marriage, I seriously considered divorce. We were just so different. I thought it wasn't going to work.

At the time of our wedding, I worked as a clothing manufacturer representative for a national men's clothing company based out of New Orleans. Wembley Industries had a showroom at the Atlanta Apparel Mart. Working out of the showroom was both good and bad. Good, because I wore the sample size of the designer fashions, but bad because I spent a lot of money on the sample size designer fashions. Good, because they sold the sample size designer fashions to me at cost, but bad because I had a closet full of those sample size gorgeous designer clothes.

After a hard day's work at the mart, I came home in my adorable pastel pink box-style top by Diane Von Furstenberg paired with a mid-calf Valentino gray pencil skirt that I bought once while taking a break at work. Influenced by Princess Diana, I wore off-white colored pantyhose with black flats and my pearl necklace. I carefully hung my clothes in the closet and dreaded my next job: making dinner.

I was drained and the tears started to flow. Who understood this dilemma of early married sacrifice? If I called my mother to discuss this problem, it would upset her, so I called a former teacher from high school who I admired and I had known long before she taught me in the classroom. This educator was about a decade older than me, who everyone loved, and whose advice was spot on. My mother taught this respected teacher when she was once a student. She was never judgmental, and I needed her wisdom at that moment.

She listened to my torment. Then she told me an anecdote of her own to help my suffering. Once in a similar position of misery, she was alone and hours away in another state from her parents. She was crying to them on the phone because she only had her two-year-old to keep her company until she made friends in her new city. Her husband was never home Monday through Friday because he traveled for his job. And there she was, too, in anguish.

Her mother comforted her for a moment then stated, "Honey, now listen. Your husband comes home tomorrow from his trip. He'll be tired. You pull yourself together and get in there and make him his favorite meal and his favorite dessert. Please stop crying! I haven't got time to talk to you right now. We can't find your father's teeth!"

Priorities.

Big Mack

*I*t's a new year and I was reminiscing about 2017. Then I started being nostalgic in general. So I pulled out my old high school yearbook and realized those are some of the most dim-witted times of our lives. The comments that people wrote in my 1971 high school album!

I went to elementary, middle, and high school with Mack Neal. He lived next door to one of my favorite girlfriends. There were lots of kids on their street. This girlfriend and I were attached at the hip. She was either at my house or I was at hers as we swapped off sleepovers on Friday nights from elementary through high school. I liked her house better because her street had more kids to hang out with, including her two-years-older sister and all her own friends. And the boys were cuter, too. We all met under the street lights until we were called in, and in the summer, that was way after dark.

This decade, the 1960s, was a more innocent time, and we all could be trusted, except for Dwayne, who was a hottie because he was really a year older but was held back a year in school, so he was not only more physically built in fifth grade, he was knowledgeable too, because he had much older brothers and sisters. His reputation preceded him. But that's another story.

One day in middle school, which we called junior high then, our teacher was absent and a male adult substituted for her. That was unusual. We mostly had female substitutes. We were respectful. There was not any misbehavior like trying to trick the sub. He called the roll to see who was in attendance, and when he reached the Ms, he called out Mack's name.

"McNeal?

Mack answered, "Present."

Present? Really? That's archaic. We used to say stuff like that.

The man said, "And what is your first name?"

Mack answered, "Mack."

The substituted responded, "What did you say? What is your first name?"

"My name is Mack Neal."

"No, son, I have your last name. What is your first name?" the man asked.

And so it went a while longer until the old man got it straight.

Now this Mack Neal and I attended school together for twelve years, played as children under that lamp post in middle school, were in the same high school classes and clubs, and were forever entwined in our small town. When he signed my favorite and precious school yearbook for the last time, I thought he would write something so profound about all our years together. I thought he would bring up memories about our adventures that I might have forgotten. I thought he respected me so much that he would write a challenge for me to make something of myself in the years to come or how he expected me to excel in this or that in my future. That's what I remember writing in his yearbook for the final time—words of wisdom, advice, some achievement in our youth that would prove that we would go far in life and make each other and our community proud.

I looked forward to seeing those sentimental and heartfelt words written only for each other in our last year of high school. It was going to be special, just like we wrote to every other person in our graduating class like, "Good Luck!" "Can't wait to get out of this place!" "Our math teacher can go to H***!"

And Mack's message to me was memorable. While reading it, I saw all the effort and thought he put into those last words that he'd probably never pen to me again, which said, "It's been real. Mack."

Must-See TV!

September 26, 2016. Are you ready for tonight's presidential debates? How are we going to stand it? But it is must-see TV! I thought of a way to make it more tolerable. I am going to turn it into a game. I first learned about this game years ago from reruns of *The Bob Newhart Show* in the afternoons. TV Land channel? I don't know. And this could be an urban legend, but the story goes that some frat boys were sitting around their fraternity house between classes in the afternoon at the time Newhart's reruns were on. Do you remember this 1970s show? I do, because I devotedly watched that fabulous lineup of comedy—Mary Tyler Moore, Bob Newhart, and then Carol Burnett on Saturday nights. When speaking to her husband, Emily Hartley, Bob's wife on the show, played by the lovely Suzanne Pleshette, seemed to always say his name in any conversation. For instance, "Where are you going, Bob?" "What do you want for dinner, Bob?" "Did you have coffee this morning already, Bob?" "Why do I always say Bob, Bob?"

So, when she spoke his name, the boys, who were drinking their beer in the social area of the house where the TV was, took a gulp. Drinking beer during the week in the afternoon? You're not surprised, are you, Bob? So, every day at the same time, when the show came on and Emily said, Bob, in her dialogue, beer was consumed.

So, I decided to tweak it. A neighborhood friend, Miss Scarlett, started coming to my house around season twenty of *The Bachelor* so that we could watch it together instead of just talking about it afterwards. For years I phoned my friend, Swoozie, who lived in another town, while the show was on. But we only talked during commercials so as not to miss a thing on the reality show. Now, with Miss Scarlett over at my house, we could talk or not while the action was taking place. We decided to play the *Bob Newhart* game. If you've ever seen *The Bachelor*, you know it's not real reality TV. It's scripted also. One way to tell is they, too, use the same verbiage over and over. Example dialogue in *every season*: "She's not here for the right reasons." "It hurts my heart to see him falling for her." "My date was amazing!" "I think we have a connection!" Those last two were really good if you wanted to get hammered.

And we must have wanted to get snockered, because once, we ended up slobbering syllables from Peach Bellinis that I made. We each had three, I hate to admit, and I am sharing the recipe.

So, tonight let's play. Want to? I know that Trump doesn't drink. His revered older brother was an alcoholic and died from it, I think, so he stays away from the stuff. What does Hillary drink? I found this out from a *Breitbart* article: "… She likes to get her drink on. Hanging out in Cartagena in 2012 with her staff at the Summit of the Americas, then-Secretary of State Clinton was photographed with her hair down and a drink in her hand. Hillary apparently outdrank Sen. John McCain (R-AZ) when they were touring Estonia in 2004. According to a witness, 'Hillary won. She stayed correct after four shots.' Terry McAuliffe, new governor of Virginia and Clinton ally, said, 'She loves to sit, throw 'em back…She's a girl from Illinois who likes to throw 'em down with the rest of us.'"

So, tonight, shots it is. The article didn't say what liquor was in her glass, so you have your choice.

What often repeated words are we listening out for and drinking to? Let me give you some help.

If Trump says: crooked, liar, show us your health physical report, not qualified.

If Clinton says: show us your tax reports, not qualified, doesn't have temperament, racist.

Take your pick and *drink up*!

Or find your own repetitive comment. Aw, hell, just drink the entire time.

Just think: Bob!

*H*ere's my recipe for Peach Bellinis:

*I*ngredients:

      2 oz peach nectar

1 tsp fresh lemon juice

1 oz peach schnapps

3 oz chilled, dry Champagne

1/2 cup crushed ice

*M*ix the peach nectar, lemon juice and schnapps in a chilled glass. Add half a cup (or more) of crushed ice, stir, and add the champagne. (Serves 2).

What Were You Expecting?

*D*ear Teachers,

Welcome back to school. Some of you are teaching for the first time. It's overwhelming to be a new teacher and being held responsible. There is *so* much you have to be accountable for these days. What's the saying? "Being a teacher is like having 1,234 tabs open on your computer." Ain't it the truth? You are all things to everybody.

I remember I was anxious those first few days of the new school year. I adorned my room with all kinds of posters pertaining to the authors that I was about to teach. There were grammar rules on signs on the walls as reminders, too. It *looked* like I knew what I was doing my first year teaching high school English. Well, I really did know my curriculum, but the students knew I was raw. This was 1979, and they planned an attack on their unfamiliar teacher who was only about six years older than they were. Let's call it, The Incident.

I had been teaching a little over a month and all seemed fine. The students and I got along well. They were well behaved. I was happy. But, the day before The Incident, I left school without deleting my notes from the chalk board. I wrote a lot of information from my lesson but had to leave fast to catch my carpool ride home with another single female teacher. In 1979, our rooms consisted of a grey or green slate board, white chalk, and dusty grey chalk erasers made of felt. Today, there are dry erase boards, dry erase markers in wonderful colors, and dry erasers. No chalk dust anywhere.

I arrived in homeroom to find my notes still visible. And since I was presenting new information to the students for first period, the board had to be erased. As I wiped the eraser across the board, there was a *whish!* A streak of fire lit up in front of my face. It was just as quick and bright as lightning! These absolutely clever, funny, creative, but would-they-get-in-big-trouble tenth-grade pupils pulled this prank by placing long matches in the creases of the eraser. When I brushed it across the board, the slate and matches connected and it lit up for a few seconds like sparklers in front of my face.

Then there was silence.

I turned around. Eyeball to eyeball, I looked at every student who was in my homeroom that morning. Some were sitting in their desks. Others were standing up, watching and waiting for my reaction. I was in disbelief. They were quietly anticipating *some* kind of penalty to be handed out at any moment. After this pause, and with them looking like deer in headlights, I said, "That was great!"

That was *not* the response they were expecting from me. And no one got in trouble.

Sincerely,

Lee "Got Away With It" St. John

P.S. I am sorry you can't have this kind of entertainment any more without reporting it—not that you might want it.

P.S.S. I just received a Facebook message from a former student from that same late 1970s class. Not only did he remember this incident, he reminded me that I used to imitate bacon frying on my desk. That is a very vague memory, but knowing me, I am sure I did. See? Now why would *the students* get in trouble if I was acting just as silly? Ah…the 1970s and our shenanigans. But as my mother used to say to me, "Something's wrong with you."

The Royal
Wedding

I am the most devoted of devoted Anglophiles. I think there is hardly anyone among my friends who say they are British Royal fanatics, too, who can outsmart me when it comes to Britain's family tree. I recently bought a 1929 Tudor revival home that we are moving into; I am an Oxfordian—look that up; and my cousin and I have researched and traced our ancestry back to the 1600s England…well, there is a kink in that line, but if there wasn't, we'd be related to someone of great importance, I just can't say who yet.

I taught British literature. I have taken *Majesty* magazine since 1981 and still continue to have a subscription. Don't try to out-English me. I know stuff. So, I guess that's how I pulled this little teaser off. My friends know about my passion. I suppose I could say all kinds of hooey and get away with it. And I did.

Mother and I shared that British publication, but it ain't cheap. It's beautifully photographed on expensive paper so if two peeps see it, it was then worth it. It has information not only on the British royals, but about the European royals as well. I've kept all the back copies and that stack is getting pretty tall. There was magazine after magazine with Princess Diana on most of the covers. Diana was a rock star and she sold magazines, right? Now, twenty years after her death, she was even seen most recently on their cover because of the anniversary of her death.

This magazine had/has the nod of approval and cooperation of the British family, so it is full of great interviews, historical information, an event calendar for each month where the royal family will be working or seen that day, and current stories better than any other magazine out there writing royal headlines.

When mother was due to give birth to me, Queen Elizabeth II's coronation was to be televised, the first ever, and it was also the world's first major international event to be broadcast on television. She worried she might give birth to me on coronation day. She was able to see it. I came along five days later.

I was so devoted to Prince Charles and Lady Diana's fairy-tale romance, that, like many others, I awoke in the early morning of July 29, 1981 to see the wedding ceremony on TV at St. Paul's Cathedral. Of course, we didn't know then what we know now. Mother and I were in London when Prince William was born on June 21, 1982. Very exciting.

When William's wedding to Catherine Middleton on April 29, 2011 at Westminster Abbey was a topic many were interested in, I decided to have a little fun with this. A month before the wedding, I wrote on my Facebook page that I was "invited to the ceremony. My invitation and ticket to enter the cathedral came in the mail today." Now, you may think this ludicrous, but Will and Kate did extend a few invitations to commoners for their upcoming nuptials. They were a modern couple wishing to modernize the monarchy by having all kinds of people represented there. And who better than this Anglophile-know-it-all? It was (un)believable. But believe some friends did.

Since I had been to Westminster Abbey, I remembered the layout. I wrote on FB my ticket told me I would be sitting in alcove E, row 17, and seat number 32. I remarked that I was "totally surprised to be one of the 'regular/commoner' guests who applied to be invited to the wedding."

My friends knew how crazed I was over the English royals, but still most knew it was a hoax. I was able to fool one social media friend. She was excited and wrote profusely to me to make sure I got every detail of the wedding so that I could relay it to her when I came home.

So, do I feel bad about this prank? Nah.

A Little Dab
Will Do Ya

I am going to let you in on a little secret. Even though I majored in public speaking as an undergraduate because I was given this gift of gab, it doesn't mean that I didn't get a little anxious before going on stage.

When I sang in my high school or church girl's trio or solo, I had butterflies and sometimes my voice cracked and I couldn't sing well. Before I went on stage for a drama performance, I was nervous and my strong voice was unusually quieter. Before I competed in some pageant, I threw up. Yes, tossed my cookies. While hovering over the toilet, I would hold my beautiful gown back with one hand and my hair with the other and give in to my nerves.

But eventually, over time, I got a little better. My inspiring co-teacher friend and I conducted many regional and state educational Gifted conferences and even one national Gifted conference during our eight years of teaching together. There were two of us, so no one was looking directly at me! She would speak while I prepped something, then I would talk while she coordinated something for the next segment, and we were never speaking alone, really. While preparing for our next individual speaking moment, we would interject something relevant here and there while the other performed. Neither of us minded. It really took the stress off of carrying the conference sessions by ourselves.

I became more comfortable leading a group of twenty, fifty, or even hundreds.

Then the money ran out. The county we worked for

couldn't afford to send us to share our lesson plans or conduct these workshops any longer and I got out of the habit of being comfortable while public speaking.

Two close friends died pretty soon after these educational speaking engagements stopped. But I was still known as someone who wouldn't mind speaking before crowds. No, I didn't mind. But giving a eulogy? All eyes were on me. There were no handouts to divert the attention away from the speaker, like at the conferences. There was no candy to throw into the audience to keep them engaged with all our infotainment. There was no overhead projector for PowerPoint slides to have them watch like we used to have while we were talking to educators. I was alone.

And nervous. This was a serious moment. I had to come up with something to get me through this.

I have this special concoction that I use on general occasions when I want to be the belle of the ball. It's called: Scotch. I take two shots. Neat. I am not a real fan of Scotch. It doesn't taste good—until the second one—and that makes it hard to swallow. But I tell you, even if I don't like it very much, it sure likes me. It must be because of my Scottish DNA. I mean, I am the darling at the party and at the funerals.

Yes, yours truly took her nerve medicine before she gave those eulogies. It just calmed me and made me relaxed enough to get the job done. And where did I take those two shots? Well, I drank those double airplane miniatures in my car after I parked in the church parking lot and away from people so I would not be seen. I would get there a little early, park far away, and down those suckers. I was chilled and in a such good frame of mind when it was my turn to speak, that after it was all over, people came up to me saying how entertaining I was. I started worrying that I might be called on to be the go-to person when someone in the future might need a speaker for funerals…that people were going to start calling me up and that I was going to have to get an agent to book all my new gigs. I was a hit because I always talked about the celebration of the person's life and made it more upbeat, thanks to the Scotch.

Now I am speaking at author engagements. And in the beginning to take the edge off, I still used my nerve medicine. It allowed me to be my uninhibited comical self. But guess what? I no longer needed to sit in a parking lot to down the elixirs. Those little Dewar's miniatures went into the buildings with me. *How?* Well, having size D bra cups, they didn't fall out. Then, all it took was a bathroom trip for just *a shot*, as now I didn't need the previously recommended dosage of two. I was weaning off my nerve medicine. If it all sounds very clandestine, well, it was!

Yes, go ahead. Be shocked! But this is what you ought to be thinking—you should be glad *you* weren't the one giving the speeches and eulogies.

Update: I've done so many speaking engagements, now my nerve medicine is no longer needed. Yay, me.

Kissin'
Cuzins

$\mathcal{I}$'ve been kissed by a president. Yep. You read that correctly.

After high school graduation and before attending college, I didn't have a summer job. I tried to enjoy those last free days before leaving home. That summer of 1971, I volunteered to help my county's chamber of commerce participate in the *Stay and See Georgia* campaign. The Georgia Department of Industry, Trade, and Tourism planned celebration activities at Lenox Square Mall, which, in 1971, was an open-air mall with breezeways connecting the stores. They planned to bring together partners in Georgia's tourism industry to showcase Georgia's assets and spread a message of *Stay and See Georgia*. Don't spend your travel dollars elsewhere. With 159 counties to choose among, they wanted travelers to stay and see what Georgia offered.

The campaign was one week long and several of us young girls manned the booth for our county. We wore our high school's matching cheerleading outfits so we would all look uniformed. The uniform top was a solid red vest with an Oxford cloth white Peter Pan collared shirt, and the sleeves came to our elbow. We had on white knee socks with still-in-my-closet Bass Saddle Oxford shoes. The knee socks had a tassel at the top fold. The skirt was mighty short. It was only as long as your fingertips by your side. The uniform had a red and black pleated plaid skirt for our school colors.

Our county's only treasure which we promoted was a Roman Catholic Church. Our Lady of the Holy Spirit

Monastery belonged to the world-wide Order of Cistercians of the Strict Observance, more commonly known as Trappists. This tourist attraction had individuals of all faiths flocking to the monastery. The monastery is sustained through The Abbey Store, a stained glass manufacturing business, a bonsai garden plant and supply business, donations, a green cemetery, and onsite retreats. One can experience this serenity of restful recollection and spiritual renewal retreat on the 2,100 acres for a day or as long as a week.

Later, in October 1990, a Conyers, Georgia homemaker by the name of Nancy Fowler claimed that the Virgin Mary appeared and instructed her to relay Mary's messages to all citizens of the United States. The directives ranged from admonitions to prayers to warnings of war. The Virgin's supposed visits made Conyers one of the longest-lived Marian apparition sites in the nation. Roads going to Mrs. Fowler's home were clogged with pilgrims yearning to hear Mary's message. Crowds as large as eighty thousand were not uncommon and Fowler had to broadcast her messages over loudspeakers. The overflow of people finally expanded from her yard to her next door pasture. There they prayed in their native tongues—English, Spanish, Russian, and Chinese—filled bottles with water from the Blessed Well, and they opened a bookstore, where they even made and sold their own bumper stickers at the store that read, *Eat, Drink, and See Mary!* Not really. But bumper stickers did exist.

Local government officials became wary of the traffic, health, and safety problems, and the Archdiocese of Atlanta became concerned that these unconfirmed visions might distract from the true faith. After 1998, pilgrimages to Conyers became less frequent.

But in 1971, we finished our week chatting with buyers at the mall and handing out brochures of information. It came to a climax when the governor's mansion held a reception for all participants. They feted us to munchies and punch for our week of hard work. We also stood in the receiving line to meet and thank our host and hostess, the Georgia governor and his wife.

Telling my aunt about our upcoming reception, she mentioned we were related—in the South, we call it kin—to Jimmy Carter. While in line, I approached the couple. I shook Rosalyn's hand first and then, when I was in front of the governor, I said, "My aunt researched our family tree and found out we are cousins." I moved on to the next person to shake his hand. From my peripheral vision, I saw Jimmy Carter leaning in closer to me and then he planted a big kiss on my cheek and said, "I always kiss my cousins!"

Telling this story years later in the 1990s to a classroom full of high school students, I prefaced my story with, "I have been kissed by a president of the United States."

Their response? "Who was it? Bill Clinton?"

Sentimental
Journey

*A*s one who likes to entertain in a humorous way, let me take a sentimental moment to write about a Christmas memory. You may find your thoughts reverting back to the late 1950s yourself. This is about a mother-daughter excursion to Rich's Department Store in Atlanta. It was a day of many thrills: eating breakfast with Santa, having pictures taken with St. Nick, flying high in the Pink Pig monorail, independently shopping in Santa's Secret Shop, and being mesmerized by the lighting of The Great Tree.

Founded in 1867, Rich's came to symbolize Atlanta's retail shopping experience during the twentieth century and was inextricably linked with our capitol's history. By the 1950s, Rich's Magnolia Tea Room Restaurant was known for its fashion shows and light luncheon fare, including their delicious chicken salad, cheese straws, and fabulous coconut cake. Our Breakfast with Santa was also held here and children squealed with delight as Santa meandered around and spoke to each of us while we enjoyed our Rice Krispies mixed with vanilla ice cream.

And I didn't spill a drop on my green velvet dress. With ruffled ankle socks and black patent leather shoes, I carried a white faux fur muff with matching hat for my picture after breakfast with St. Nick. Although lines were long, I was never frightened because he looked just like the picturesque Coca-Cola Santa. Photographs were taken while children sat on his knee and whispered their secret Christmas desires. Santa's helpers gave green Christmas tree-shaped candy to partakers. The black-and-white five-by-seven photo was mailed to your home shortly after your visit.

Another thrill was riding Priscilla, The Pink Pig. In 1956, the bright pink monorail debuted with a piggy snout and curly tail. This magical journey around the toy department with all the toys, decorations, and sparkling lights was only three and a half minutes long, costing a quarter. Later moving to the rooftop, the car traveled onto the Crystal Bridge, a four-story all-glass bridge that stretched across Forsyth Street, connecting Rich's two buildings. It then carried you around the base of the tree, giving an enormous view of all the glistening ornaments as large as basketballs and a view overlooking the city streets. I still have a white, satin sticker with Priscilla's smiling face declaring, *I Rode the Pink Pig.*

I remember shopping at Santa's Secret Shop on the fifth floor. The emporium allowed me to privately pick out inexpensive gifts for my parents because adults were not allowed in. Santa's elves assisted me while Mother shopped elsewhere in the store. Rich's set up accounts where parents paid for their children's acquisitions using what was called the charge plate. All purchases were secretly wrapped.

As the day stretched into dusk, Mother and I, along with tens of thousands from all over the South, attended the lighting of The Great Tree. Generating more anticipation for the ceremony, city lights were turned off for about thirty minutes after a complete sunset. Then the freshly-cut seventy-five-foot-tall Georgia White pine came to life with its miles of sparkle and seven-foot-tall star. Standing atop the Crystal Bridge, each of the bridge's four levels provided Christmas carols from heralding choruses. Rich's Great Tree was featured on the cover of *Time* magazine on December 15, 1961.

Everything about Rich's was ours. It was home, and not

just at Christmas. It was as much a part of the Atlanta land-scape as the statue of the Phoenix—purchased by Rich's—once featured downtown and known as "Atlanta from the Ashes," a symbol of Atlanta's revival. This Christmas memory's afterglow warms me since this tradition at this location no longer exists. But once there was a time that was magical and Southerners came near and far to spend a part of their holiday at "The Store of the South."

Toot, Toot

I am a *Seinfeld* junkie. Here's one of his best: "To me, the thing about birthday parties is that the first birthday party you have and the last birthday party you have are actually quite similar. You know, you just kinda sit there…you're the least excited person at the party. You don't even really realize that there is a party."

He also says that with the first birthday party, which you don't know what is happening, your parents are telling you, "These are your friends." It's the same with the last birthday party, especially if you are the oldest, and I mean really oldest, in the room—say you made it to your tenth decade. What friends do you really have left? The ones invited, you are told, "These are your friends," which you probably don't know who they are either.

Another relevance with the beginning until the end of life is—and how can I put it delicately—the bodily function, BM. Do I have to define it? My family calls it a toot. Do you have a word for it, too? I don't think we called anything of the human physical condition by the scientific name. So, I am going to call it a toot, too.

Toots are foremost on the mind of new parents. They keep up with how often and how well the baby is tooting. It is symbolic of how irritated or comfortable the baby might be so you can plan a little about what to expect from the unexpected. Not only that, but you have to be able to describe the toot. That's another indicator of the baby's well-being. As the child grows, it's all about the bathroom schedule as well.

"Make sure you go to the bathroom before we leave!" "Did you go to the bathroom? They may not have one when we get there." Bathroom, bathroom, bathroom. And it's not just about the toot. You might have to urinate, or as we called it, tee-tee. Yes, my husband and adult sons still call it tee-tee.

Finally, you think for yourself and do not have to be reminded because you've learned some lesson along the way...like the time you were in Germany and instead of seeing all the sights you'd planned, you had to take some off the list because you've added all the public restrooms in that area to your trip.

Later, you deal with all your pets. You concentrate on "watering" the dog or timing their eating habits to coincide with toot relief in the morning, during the day, and your evening stroll. Their body excretions need to be met with regularity for their comfort and your schedule, so, even though your kids are grown, you can't catch a break because of your pets' needs.

And then, it's your turn once more. Again, it's all about how well and regular one is and what you can and cannot eat for the right outcome. Can't we concentrate on something else? Do we worry about our teeth falling out, or how we will eventually smell to young people, and do we need to bathe every day since we didn't do much for a day or two? But having a BM is foremost on many minds.

"Birthdays are merely symbolic of how another year has gone by and how little we've grown," Jerry Seinfeld's character once said in an episode of the Show About Nothing. "No matter how desperate we are that someday a better self will emerge, with each flicker of the candles on the cake, we know it's not to be—that for the rest of our sad, wretched, pathetic lives, this is who we are to the bitter end. Inevitably, irrevocably. Happy birthday? No such thing."

Vivisepulture

*I*f you were not able to attend the TombTails & ArtFest Oak Hill Cemetery Tour on Saturday, October 14, you missed an early Halloween treat—pun intended. Storytellers and guides captivated guests with lively, engaging tales while dancers, musicians, and artists contributed to this yearly event that celebrated living, history, and the arts.

For my part, I hosted a stopover to discuss vivisepulture. What the heck is that? If you are a young reader, you must stop now and get permission from your parents to continue reading. The remainder of this article is rated PG-13. Go ask your parents if you may continue. I'll wait.

Okay. You're back.

Vivisepulture means being buried alive. Taphophobia means the fear of being buried alive. Maybe you are asking how someone could be buried alive and why there would be a fear of it. Before the twentieth century's established death identification, and before there was embalming, The London Association for the Prevention of Premature Burial was established in 1896. There was such a fear of being buried alive that many preventive measures were taking place in the nineteenth century to prevent it.

People fell into comas and such that were misunderstood by doctors, who pronounced them dead. The story I relayed at my stop dealt with a young Argentinian woman who was buried once but died twice. In 1902, this young woman was getting ready to enjoy her nineteenth birthday when she lost consciousness and collapsed. Three doctors declared her dead. She was placed in a coffin, given a funeral, and sealed in a tomb. A few days later, according to legend, a cemetery worker noticed that the coffin had moved. Suspecting a grave robber, he opened the casket and discovered scratch marks on the inside. Buried alive, she awakened in her tomb and attempted to escape by smashing and scratching the lid before she died of cardiac arrest.

If doctors were getting this all wrong in the 1800s, how else could a pre-mature burial be prevented? Their solutions were to keep bodies in mortuaries for an extended period until the beginning of putrefaction so as to make sure the person really was dead. Or they established hospitals for the dead to wait it out in the same way. To deal with it, they placed loads of flowers around the beds of dead patients. There was once a location called the Apparent Dead House, where they placed feathers or mirrors under the nose of a person to check for breathing. A disgusting practice, they also used to test for signs of life among the apparent dead by giving tobacco smoke enemas. This was mostly practiced in Europe in the late 1800s. Smoke—blown through a pipe into the rectum—was thought to bring people back from the brink of death. Maybe that's where the saying, "Blowing smoke up my a**'" came from.

If there was still any doubt, they created safety coffins for the dead. They tied a string around the deceased's finger that was inserted through a hole in the coffin and up through the ground in a tube and again tied above ground to a bell hanging on a hook. If the person came back from the dead, they could ring the bell for the cemetery watchman making rounds day or night. Such sayings from this invention were "dead ringer," "saved by the bell," and "graveyard shift." Those buried in vaults used spring-loaded lids to crawl out.

However, there are no such reported cases of the left-for-dead being saved by such contraptions.

The thought and fear of being buried alive encouraged Edgar Allan Poe to write the short story *The Premature Burial* in 1844 about a man being obsessed with the idea of falling into a trance and mistakenly interred.

With our modern-day science, we do not have this fear. We have others. And as Jerry Seinfeld said, and I paraphrase, the number one fear these days is public speaking. Number two is death. So, a person would rather be in the coffin than giving the eulogy.

F – Failure or Fantastic?
You Decide

My preschool—you know that had to be a long time ago!—teacher's genius son ended up at MIT and founded another part of the atom in the 1950s. I once heard that when he was in first grade, he received an F on a report card. When he brought this information home, he asked his mother, "What does F mean?" She remarked, "It means you are fantastic!" She couldn't bring herself to tell him what it really meant because, after all, he was just six.

I have a long resume of teaching gigs: church preschool, church adult Sunday School, public elementary school, home school, public middle school, public high school, summer school, and public night school.

My night school job was eye-opening. Thank goodness for a somewhat, last, chance for some students. Those who make the most of it, I congratulate you! But for those who are there—and why else would they be there if they aren't trying to better themselves?—please don't disrupt my trying to teach you something.

I learned later that I had a female student who was in my night school class because she was previously dismissed from her other county's school system for throwing a desk at someone. I think that someone was a teacher. Thanks for the heads-up!

I tried to make the American literature lessons relevant. I really did. One student obediently came to class every night, sat quietly as a mouse, and failed every test. When he didn't pass the class, he spoke to me for the first time—although I did try to prompt him to contribute to the discussion in class to little success. He asked me why he made an F. I answered that 1) he made an F on every test and 2) there was not much contribution in the class discussions for me to be able to determine he was absorbing the material for him to pass. I couldn't tell what he knew. He responded, "But I came to class every night!" I countered by saying, "Would I use a doctor who never missed a medical lecture but still made Fs on all his exams? Would you have a doctor operate on you under those conditions?"

He was a really nice guy, and I hated to drop that news on him, but I certainly couldn't give him something without some signs of comprehension. I wanted to. But my conscience wouldn't let me. It wouldn't be fair to those who did work for it. I felt terrible for him.

Gosh, it's hard on the students these days. I am not being sarcastic either. It really is. All the demands they and others put on themselves. They need to remember this: more C-average college students become CEOs of corporations. They have learned how to balance fun and grades.

My good friend, Swoozie, works for a public school test prep company whose website vision states:

PRACTICE MAKES PERFECT
With lots of opportunities to review and practice concepts and skills, Common Core Performance Coach is the program that will pave the path to success on the new high-stakes assessments.

The program allows teachers to implement lessons in a variety of ways and can reinforce Common Core Coach instruction or supplement any other program. Many examples are provided in order to solidify understanding. Practice tests

*mirror question types that will be seen in the new assessments
and simulates in paper format what students will see online.*

*Common Core Performance Coach is perfect for ongoing
instruction throughout the year or more intensive instruction
and test prep before the tests.*

*S*he recently received a phone call while at work.
The name that popped up on her phone screen read,
Jesus, and she was nervous for a moment that Jesus was
calling and wondered should she answer it. After rational-
izing that and calming down, she answered and heard a young
male voice say very softly, "Can I speak to the manager?"
She replied, "I'm the manager. Can I help?" He commented,
"I'm in class right now and I need the answers to the test your
company provides."

She replied, "I am sorry but we don't provide answers to
students." He said, "Thank you" and hung up. Using his cell
phone in class, he must have found her company's website
and called for help!

Some things change, and then again, some things don't.
He was so polite...and I bet he even showed up to class
every day.

Grading Papers
Leftover Laughter from the Classroom

*N*ow that I am a retired teacher, I don't miss reading and editing all those essays. One reason is because I am editing all of my essays for my books, my blogs, the newspaper, or when I guest blog. But I came across this ditty that somehow found its way into a pile I needed to discard. What a fiasco this writing was. Prior to retiring in Coweta County, I also taught in Cobb, DeKalb, and Rockdale. I am not telling you which county this student attended.

This was their prompt: Much thought has gone into Shakespeare's *Romeo and Juliet* as star-crossed lovers. It is unique among Shakespeare's tragedies because it seems to be fate, not character that seals their doom. Agree or disagree with this statement citing specific scenes and quotations to support your stance. Since this is a timed test, you have 75 minutes to support your case.

For your reading, I corrected some of the punctuation to have it make more sense, if that is possible. Here is one student's take:

*T*hat the great William Shakespeare's famous book, *Romeo and Juliet*, (which I might add is one of my personal favorites) is not so much about it being about character or fate because one could easily agree with that statement or disagree with it. Is it about character? Or is it about fate? The real answer to this statement has a great deal to do with how Shakespeare might have felt about "character" or "fate."

Certainly, as the world's most famous writer, Shakespeare himself must have had some thought on "character" or "fate." What were his feelings about these young people's character? Or does he lean more to the thought that Romeo and Juliet were held captive by their own fate? While other fine books by Shakespeare are also called tragedies, is *Romeo and Juliet*, a book I enjoyed reading and rereading, really a tragedy?

To prove one point or the other, one must find (by citing) the specific scenes and quotations in Romeo and Juliet. But these quotations and scenes are too numerous to mention in this timed essay. If time permits, I will specify them at the end.

There is no reason to believe Shakespeare himself was ever involved in star-crossed activities. He may have been but our teacher did not provide that information while teaching this book so I cannot argue that point in this paper. If I had that information, I would have provided it here. As I didn't, I cannot. That is okay because this is a timed test and with everything else I have to write about, I doubt I would have had time to put that information in this writing test that we are taking. I mean, it is one thing to talk about Romeo or Juliet's fate as star-crossed lovers but quite another to add that the playwright might have been subjected to fate, also. Who knows?

She did tell us that the musical *West Side Story* is derived from this book by Shakespeare. I remember she showed us that movie and the fire escape symbolized the balcony scene in the *Romeo and Juliet* movie that we also watched. Although it was in black and white, it was pretty good.

I only have ten more minutes until my time is up. Because of the time constraints on this essay, it has been difficult to prove or disprove the statement about character or fate, although it will always be one of my favorite books that we read this year. I wish I had more time because there are so many wonderful references that should be brought up in this paper and I would if...

ime!

Take Me Out to the
Ballgame

*B*aseball is all around us and the temps are cooperating. But here comes the pollen. Still, spring has sprung and that means America's pastime is "at bat."

Some may argue that today, football, not baseball, is America's National Pastime. But in the first half of the twentieth century, there was no question that baseball was America's sport. I am proud as punch to say my father was an outstanding baseball player in college at Oglethorpe University in Atlanta. He also played for the Chicago Cubs organization. But before all this, he played on a high school traveling team in 1932, when this story takes place.

His team played anybody who would host them. And in the late spring of 1932, they were in Atlanta playing some of the guards at the Atlanta Penitentiary while a few inmates were allowed to watch. There was one game when my dad, a left-handed pitcher, played in the outfield. While playing center field, he kept stepping farther and farther into the backfield. Just a little at a time so as to not draw attention doing so. He kept inching back because he saw two men sitting on some bleachers and he wanted to ask them a question. He had heard there was a certain high-profile inmate in the Atlanta Pen and wanted to find out if it was true. So, little by little, meandering towards the bleachers, he got close enough to turn around and ask if this infamous person was indeed incarcerated there.

He circled around to ask quickly as he didn't want it to

seem he was not paying attention to the game and his position. Was this American gangster, boss of the Chicago Outfit and famous Prohibition era badass really there? Was this crime boss, with a seven-year reign of smuggling and bootlegging liquor, in the building? Was this man, who was in a league of his own terrorizing Chicago during Prohibition in the 1920s and who was convicted of tax evasion in 1931, now an inmate in Atlanta's prison?

This gangster was sent to the Atlanta U.S. Penitentiary in May 1932. At 250 pounds, he was officially diagnosed with syphilis and gonorrhea. He suffered from withdrawal symptoms from cocaine addiction and his use of this drug had perforated his septum. He was competent at his prison job of stitching the soles on shoes for eight hours a day, yet he was barely coherent when writing his letters. At the Atlanta Pen, he was seen as a weak personality and was just not the mobster from which his legend was made. He was so out of his depth dealing with the bullying fellow inmates inflicted that his cellmate feared this thug would have a nervous breakdown. When Alcatraz Federal Penitentiary opened, he was moved there.

So, Daddy was curious. Was he still there? Backing his way to the bleachers, he was close enough now to turn around to ask the two men sitting there watching the game if Alphonse Gabriel "Al" Capone was in the Atlanta Penitentiary.

One of the two answered, "He sure is, and he's sitting right here next to me."

I Am a Sucker!

I am a sucker for all those tests that show up online, mostly on Facebook, that can tell your Intellectual Quotient, your Emotional Quotient, your aura color, your top personality traits, which movie star you look like, what literary character you are most like, etc., all in ten to twenty questions. I'm a S-U-C-K-E-R.

I have the highest Facebook IQ, the most tenderhearted EQ, every color of the rainbow when I retake that color test for the tenth time to get a color I want because I answer the questions differently each time trying to score my favorite color, such a great personality I should run for office, am Grace Kelly's doppelganger, a Scarlett O'Hara literary heroine, and can score 20 on a scale of 1-10. I might as well be a Barbie doll because she's so perfect.

Barbie is every career from a model to doctor. She is vintage, yet fashionable. She dresses for all the holidays and still wears a spacesuit. She is thin and yet can be curvy. She is every ethnicity. She is the darling of the seas as Ariel or she can fly on a magic carpet like Jasmine. She is expensive but also frugal. She wears designer Mattel clothes but also wears homemade frocks from Amazon, Etsy, or your favorite seamstress. She is a collector but some throw her away after her hair tangles. She might like to have a boyfriend but doesn't need one. And she has a fast pink convertible. This girl rocks.

According to my online tests, I am as fantastic as she.

And it only took a minute to answer all the questions because they were all multiple choice.

You know about multiple-choice tests, don't you? They have a stem, a correct answer, a keyed alternative, and distractors. The stem presents the item as a problem to be solved, a question asked of the respondent, or an incomplete statement to be completed, as well as any other relevant information.

Middle schools used to have aptitude tests. The counselors gave these tests to gain insight into the kinds of jobs/careers students could be thinking about for their future. They gave these tests before high school so that pupils could plan on what courses they should take for either the college-prep course track diploma or the technical-track diploma.

The test was dead-on when it came to my first child's innate ability. His prognosis indicated that he was good with his hands. He is now assistant director for the learning environments of labs, classroom, and collaborative spaces for Georgia State University. Fancy name for he works in IT and uses his hands.

But I think what I worry a little about is the girl who sat next to him in his eighth-grade classroom. When the results came in, she told our oldest child her test results. I wonder what she is doing today. Her test results told her she should either become a clown…or a mime.

I Am a
Tooth
Grinder

I don't know when it started, but, of course, like many, I needed to eventually get a mouth guard. Mouth guards are coverings worn over teeth, and often used to protect teeth from injury from teeth grinding and during sports.

According to *WebMD*, there are three types:

"Stock mouth protectors are preformed and come ready to wear. They are inexpensive and can be bought at most sporting goods stores and department stores. However, little can be done to adjust their fit, they are bulky, make breathing and talking difficult, and they provide little or no protection. Dentists do not recommend their use.

"Boil and bite mouth protectors also can be bought at many sporting goods stores and may offer a better fit than stock mouth protectors. The boil and bite mouth guard is made from thermoplastic material. It is placed in hot water to soften, then placed in the mouth and shaped around the teeth using finger and tongue pressure.

"Custom-fitted mouth protectors are individually designed and made in a dental office or a professional laboratory based on your dentist's instructions. First, your dentist will make an impression of your teeth and a mouth guard is then molded over the model using a special material. Due to the use of the special material and because of the extra time and work involved, this custom-made mouth guard is more expensive than the other types, but it provides the most comfort and protection.

"Generally, mouth guards cover your upper teeth only, but in some instances (such as if you wear braces or another fixed dental appliance on your lower jaw), your dentist will make a mouth guard for the lower teeth as well. Your dentist can suggest the best mouth guard for you. An effective mouth guard should be comfortable, resist tears, be durable and easy to clean, and should not restrict your breathing or speech.

"If you grind your teeth at night, a special mouth guard-type of dental appliance, called a nocturnal bite plate or bite splint, may be created to prevent tooth damage."

I had the third kind, the custom fit night thingy one. It only covered my front two teeth, just enough to keep my bite open.

Over time, years really, I ground it down until it broke. Now, this guard isn't cheap. Hopefully, they kept my mold, but if not, I was going to have to pay for that, too. And I didn't want to have to fork out that kind of money.

So, as usual, I came up with my own grind solution. I bought a baby pacifier. I mean, all I really needed was something between my teeth to keep the grinding at bay. A pacifier is used for soothing and comforting a fussy baby. Sucking often provides a soothing, calming effect for a baby. I didn't need it for sucking, of course. I needed it to keep my mouth open a little so my teeth didn't touch during the night.

So, I bought one. Still have it. Still use it on occasion. It stays in the top drawer of my bed's nightstand.

But I just found out about this from *Baby Pants*:

"Baby Pants Classic Adult pacifiers are larger versions of the ever popular Gerber NUK pacifiers. The shield is approximately 2 5/8 inch wide and 1 7/8 tall. The nipple extends 1 5/8 inch from the shield. The nipple shape is identical to the NUK 5 but slightly larger. The size makes them ideal for easy stress free sucking all night. They stay in place without effort. For use by ages 13 and older."

I'll have to see about that.

I Don't
Want to Grow Up

*A*fter the loss of several pounds in six months because of not providing my body with as many alcohol calories as I had previously supplied it, I wondered if I was still fun. Remember the alcohol loosens me up for mayhem behavior. Whatever I thought about doing, there was no filter in my actions because of those elixirs. But I am glad to report I've still got it. Here's the latest.

Shopping on the last Saturday before Christmas weekend, my younger-teacher-friend asked me to go with her to Atlanta. Because she had just gotten out of school for winter break, she was behind on her shopping and had to get some things done. I wouldn't think anyone would really want shop for Christmas presents on the last Saturday in Atlanta if they didn't have to. But she had to and she asked me to tag along.

As a retiree, I didn't have to go. Not only were my presents bought, they were already distributed to the recipients, and opened by them, too, I might add. But that's a luxury of retirement; don't wish you could have this much time to be finished early with Christmas responsibilities. Remember, retirement is for *old* people. If you are younger than retirement age, don't wish it away.

I mostly decided to tag along to be with her, of course, but also to see how the malls were decorated. I hadn't been in a mall in years. I tend to shop in the standalone businesses, online, or create some food for the recipient and their family to enjoy. So, getting out and visiting the pretty sights, even with all the humanity, which I was going to try to ignore—

yeah, right—was going to be entertaining. And she was driving in that Atlanta traffic. I wasn't in charge of anything. I was along for the ride.

We started early and arrived home after dark. She was on a mission, and I don't blame her. Her job was to get 'er done. I recently had a bit of plantar fasciitis. I knew I might need to sit down on our walking/shopping excursion to keep it at bay. And I did. So it wasn't so much the standing and walking on our excursion as it was the length of the all-day mission trip. But I signed up for it.

Late in the day, I was starting to be worn slap out. By that I mean standing in those long lines and the slow tick-tick-ticking of the minutes before it was our turn to make a purchase, especially at Bath and Body Works in Perimeter Mall, became tiresome.

Younger-teacher-friend needed several items from there as gifts. She is such a girlie girl, even if she has an entire household of testosterone. There were three lines and the wait looked unbearable. But instead of both of us in line, I suggested she continue shopping while I hold her place for her to cut the time on the wait. The lines barely moved. They must have hired a bunch of new people for Christmas to run the register. It didn't look like they had the ringing-up of the merchandise rhythm down yet.

So, while waiting, I, of course, started talking to others in line to pass the time. Time stood still just like for all the purchasers and I tried to make the best of it. I didn't mind holding her place, it would have been worse to shop and line up later. She soon joined me and we still had a ways to go. It's like the saying, "hurry up to slow down." You know the feeling. Anyway, we both were chatting away with our fellow shoppers when I started to become giddy. When I get bored, watch out!

I started using my outside voice. That's what we called it when I taught preschool. We had inside voices and outside voices. With my outside voice, I was taking command. I talked loudly so others could hear me say, "Did everyone get their number? You need a number to be called to purchase your gift." Or, "Don't forget to get your number before you get in line." Then, very loudly, I started calling out numbers, "Number twenty-six," "Number seventy-nine," and so on. That was really fun to watch their faces then. Because it was so crowded, only those around me knew the source of this outlandishness and giggled...or were amusingly horrified, which I knew they were because of the expression on their faces. Then, getting closer to our destination, which was the sales counter, I continued and said, "After your purchase, be sure and get your ticket stub stamped for free parking." There wasn't a ticketed garage or a parking attendant to pay at the mall. But I yelled that out to appear so. It was the last thing I remember saying as we walked out of the store. And I said it several times to continue watching the reactions to amuse myself with my trickery.

Thank goodness my younger-teacher-friend did not mind and laughed along as we left the store. My partner-in-crime from my younger days would have done the same back then. But today, when I act goofy while visiting her in her Atlanta suburb, she shames me. She has grown up now, I guess. She says, "You can't act like that up here." What? Am I supposed to pretend I am mature?

I'm not.

You Better
Watch Out,
You Better Not Cry...

hen The Heir was five years old, I decided to make his Christmas really special. We mothers will go to any lengths to create memories around holidays. Sure, I'd done the cookie and milk trick, home-made, left on a Christmas designed plate, with a carrot for Rudolf, but this year was going to be different.

When we tucked him in and he fell asleep, I pulled out from my bedroom closet my husband's L.L. Bean boots. In Georgia, I doubt those boots were worn more than a half dozen times each winter because of our mild temperatures. If we were lucky, it might snow twice during the season, but we were ready in case it did. I had a pair, too. Made in Maine, the boots were originally designed by the company's founder, L.L. Bean, in 1912. The style has never changed and the company touts they are so well built that "Chances are, you'll only ever need one pair."

With these boots I had also stashed ahead of time several of the largest size baking soda boxes that the grocery stores carried. Quietly taking the boots and baking soda to the living room, I laid down a boot on the rug, poured baking soda around the perimeter, lifted the boot, placed the matching boot a step ahead, and again poured the baking soda. After several times, it looked as if Santa had sloughed off snow on his way from our fireplace to our Christmas tree to deliver the presents.

Our fireplace stood empty because we didn't use it. We

had a cast iron red enamel wood burning stove sitting on our hearth. We didn't crank up that stove all that much in the South either. But when temperatures dropped, we did, and the glow from the deep red enamel and watching the flames through the glass doors while hearing the sound of crackling wood burning was mesmerizing. At Christmas, you can imagine it really set the mood. The warmth it emitted blanketed the entire house. But the fact that our chimney was blockaded by that huge wood burning stove should have been a clue that Santa would have trouble maneuvering around that contraption in the fireplace. But our first born was five, and being my dreamer child, he wouldn't have thought about all the pipes standing in Santa's way as he descended.

Christmas morning arrived and The Heir jumped out of bed, ran into the living room, saw all the presents, and was excited and impressed when he saw Santa's footsteps left behind on the rug. His eyes widened. He was so overjoyed that Santa had been in his house!

Our usual festivities of opening all the presents ensued and friends and more family popped over later that day and *for several days after* to see what The Heir received from St. Nick. Our son bragged to them all about Santa's arrival and could prove it: "See, there are his footprints. They are still here!" He proudly continued to show them off for days after.

Nailed it.

Being so pleased about my cleverness and our oldest son's excitement, when The Spare turned five, I thought I'd recreate the same scenario again. The oldest son was now thirteen so we had to make sure he kept his adventure a secret so his younger brother could have as much fun as he enjoyed regarding Santa's clandestine visit.

Christmas morning came again. This time, it was The

Spare who ran into the living room where our tree stood with numerous wrapped gifts under and around it, paused, looked at the setting where Santa would have had to come into our home from the night before to deliver all those presents, and the first thing out of his mouth was, "Why hasn't it melted?"

Secret Agent

I have been playing bridge now for about eight years. When I say "playing," I really play *at* it. It is a very hard game to maneuver. It's harder than Old Maids. It's even harder than Go-Fish, which means it's a pretty hard game to grasp.

It was created by a Vanderbilt, for crying out loud. Well, it wasn't really created by a Vanderbilt, but one improved it. The history of contract bridge may be dated as early as the sixteenth century. Contract bridge is just what it means, you enter into a bidding contract with your partner. Harold Stirling Vanderbilt changed the rules from the former game into what it is today. I'll spare you from having to hear all those archaic rules of yesteryear. I'll even save you from hearing about the rules that have been in place since 1925.

It is the second most popular card game in the world. It can be a serious tournament game, duplicate bridge, or you can play it for fun socially, kitchen bridge/social bridge. It is always challenging. Bill Gates said, "Bridge is the King of all games."

Oh, the joy of playing bridge. Someone once said, "Playing duplicate bridge is the ultimate social game for thinkers." I like, "Kitchen bridge has a great sense of *rumor.*" Get the picture? What would you rather have? Seriousness or fun? I suppose a golfer has the same quandary. One wants to seriously play well, but, on the other hand, wants to have fun doing it. Of course, it is fun winning at bridge, but you are in a nightmare sometimes until you do. If you have the slightest touch of masochism, you'll love this game.

After the cards are dealt, players place them from high to low, sometimes low to high, in their particular suit. Some ladies from my neighborhood bridge club came down to the lake to play cards one weekend and I ran to the restroom while the cards were being dealt. I returned, picked up my cards to organize them in my hand, and that step was already completed. Had anyone touched my cards? *No!* They were in perfect order from high to low by suit and high to low by number. *Creepy.* What are the statistical chances of that happening? I should have played the lottery that week.

Here's the thing about bridge which absolutely cracks me up: there are codes. You and your partner are bidding, coding back and forth, and your opponents are just decoding as fast as you bid them. I mean, why can't one gal say, "I have an equal amount of cards from each suit, my total points equal between fourteen and sixteen, and I want to know what my partner's best five-card suit is in her hand."

Instead, this is what is said: "One-no trump." Now that answer is not so bad. But it's the responses that get me. In kitchen bridge, one can just ask, "Are we playing Jacoby?" But in duplicate bridge, you had better know that convention because one can't talk. Then when Jacoby play is established, the bid turns into something else altogether which is known by everyone at the table! So, what's with all the secret codes? If Jacoby is out in the open, there is no secret in the bidding after that.

There are other secrets to bridge that everyone knows about. If you play Blackwood or Gerber conventions codes, you're asking your partner for how many aces and kings they have. They answer in a bid that everyone knows, and so it goes. So, what's the big deal with trying to be discreet and yet everyone playing at the table knows what kind of cards you have?

Forget being a good sleuth and thinking you are some secret agent discovering hidden bidding clues in bridge. *Everyone* knows. But here's a clue: Eye Donut Kerr.

"Miss Right"
or
"Miss Right Now"?

*O*ver the years, June has been the traditional month for weddings. Hubby and I recently attended a destination wedding in Highlands, North Carolina. Destination weddings are hot, and I don't mean as in temperature. Maybe they always have been, but it seems more so these days.

With the evening wedding ceremonies conducted and the reception fun over, the "old timers" had some down time the next morning at a brunch for the out-of-town guests. We shared memories of how we first met our spouses. The groom's dad told this one about a friend of his:

A college buddy was enjoying the fruits of youthful behavior at a local bar in Atlanta with other carousing friends. They were having such a good time, in fact, that one of the guys fell off a barstool and broke his leg.

Luckily for them, Piedmont Hospital was just down Peachtree Street, so they gathered up this broken friend, placed him in the car, and headed for the hospital's emergency entrance. While there, they rose to the occasion and answered all questions posed by the doctors on call about the accident. They were serious and forthcoming about the details of the incident.

But when their injured pal was admitted to the back room for more examinations, they were left out of that trip and were waiting around in the hospital emergency room lobby for more news regarding their companion. These young bucks had responsibly done their duty and all that was left of them was to wait it out and bring their friend home. So, what would some young men, after a night of drinking, do to kill time in a hospital waiting room?

They all started flirting with the nurses.

Groom's dad's friend was especially enamored with one of the RNs on duty. Even though she was working, he chatted with her when he could during her night shift. He thought he made a good impression but knew he couldn't make a real move because she was busy.

So, the next day, he called the hospital, was put through to the emergency room, asked whoever answered the phone to help him find this adorable gal he had met and tried to impress. He gave the caller her description in detail, or what he remembered. The medical assistant on the phone said, "Oh, Nurse Betty? Yes, she was on duty here last night."

He asked to speak to her. Eventually, she was able to answer the phone and talk to this smitten young man. He flirted some more using his witty words and asked her if she remembered their conversation from the night before. He was sure she would recall their exchange because he had done his best to make an impression. Yet, she didn't. She explained that it was a very busy night at the hospital and she just didn't recollect some of the things he was reiterating.

He wanted to meet her and he asked if they could get together for a drink at Harrison's on Peachtree Street, ironically, the bar where the accident occurred. He described what he would be wearing so she could find him easily.

The nurse walked in, saw this young man by his depiction, sat down at his table, and the first words out of his mouth were, "You're the wrong one."

He and "the wrong one" have been married over forty years.

Bonjour!

Bonjour!
    Pourquoi ai-je prendre des cours de français au secondaire? Ce qu'il a été bon pour moi? Bien sûr, je peux aller dans un restaurant français et dire, Garçon! quand je veux commander un verre d'eau, mais la lecture du menu? It ain't gonna get moi très loin.

Translation: Why did I take French in high school? What good has it been to me? Sure, I can go into a French restaurant and say, Garçon! when I want to order a glass of water, but reading the menu? It ain't gonna get me very far.

See? After taking French I and II in high school and a year in college, this is what it amounts to. Oh, I've even been to Paris…twice. It's a beautiful romance language but they weren't very impressed when I spoke the little French I did remember, which was: "french fries," "french dressing," and "french kissing." And I am also crazy about country french décor. Maybe this appreciation for all things French comes from my DNA. I am a descendent of French Huguenots on my maternal grandfather's side.

Sometimes I become giddy and just break out into a French accent for the fun of it. And although in my head it sounds like the native tongue, I know it comes out just like Pepe le Pew, the fictional cartoon character from the Warner Brother's *Looney Tunes* and *Merri Melodies*. First introduced in 1945, le Pew is depicted as a French skunk constantly in search of love. But his offensive odor and aggressiveness in the pursuit of romance causes other characters to flee from him in fear while he hops after them in leisurely pursuit.

Pepe Le Pew's storylines typically involve his quest of a female black cat, Penelope Pussycat, whom he mistakes for a skunk—la belle femme skunk fatale. This black cat squeezed under a newly painted fence and is unaware that wet white paint caused a white stripe down her back. Of course, this attracts Le Pew, but every time he tries to embrace her, she frantically races to get away from him because of his putrid odor. He never loses confidence no matter how many times he is rebuffed. These escapades are always set in exotic locales in France associated in popular culture with romance, such as the Champs-Elysees or the Eiffel Tower.

And zee? Ah con speek jus liake hem.

Once, when putting my best French forward, I made a rather funny faux pas. In the summer of 1976, I was working at the Omni International Hotel in Atlanta, answering the phone for the catering department. The hotel's main restaurant prepared French cuisine. Hors d'oeuveres were *délicieux*. Des salades were *magnifique*. Entrees were *attrait*. Desserts were *exquisite*.

When the phone rang, I answered and a woman on the other end said, "Hello. Could you please read the list of the entrée choices in the main restaurant tonight?"

When I started reading from the poisson section a delicious favorite stood out. The recipe's name, according to French lore, is referenced to a miller of wheat whose wife cooked everything coated with flour. The original French style of cooking this fish, then, was seasoned and floured, sautéed in butter, and finally topped with the brown butter from the pan. It was listed on the menu as Trout Meunière, which with my haste and poor French skills, I delivered as *trout manure*.

Tales from the Crypt

*I*n 4022, Howard Carson needed a change. He had just failed in his latest experiment which involved camel hump productivity. To help him in his misery, he decided to run a marathon. While on his run, he fell into a hole which landed him smack into the hallway of the Motel of the Mysteries, one of the greatest discoveries of modern times. Upon further investigation, he found the ancient world of Usa. "Imagine, then, the excitement that Howard Carson, an amateur archeologist at best, experienced when in crossing the perimeter of an abandoned excavation site he felt the ground give way beneath him and found himself at the bottom of a shaft, which, judging from the *Do Not Disturb* sign hanging from an archaic doorknob, was clearly the entrance to a still-sealed burial chamber. Carson's incredible discoveries, including the remains of two bodies, one of them on a ceremonial bed facing an altar that appeared to be a means of communicating with the Gods and the other lying in a porcelain sarcophagus in the Inner Chamber, permitted him to piece together the whole fabric of that extraordinary civilization."

He learned that in 1985, North America was decimated by a monumental catastrophe involving mail and the collapse of the ozone layer. In his dig, he uncovered various monuments, some writing fragments, and with other researchers was able to expose, decipher, and identify through tagging the chambers' secrets and their purpose from a long-forgotten late twentieth century society.

Here were his descriptions from this underground treasure trove of archeological finds while in the Inner-Most Sanctum of the Inner Chamber:

1. The Sacred Urn – this object was located in the Inner Sanctum of the Inner Chamber. He determined its use to be where one knelt on one's knees, leaned over its wide openness, and chanted into the flushing waters after its lever was pulled downward.

2. The Sacred Collar – this paper strip, thin in density but wide enough to strap around the urn lid, was usually anchored to the Sacred Urn.

3. The Sacred Headband – Carson decided the urn lid should have a name because although it was secured to the Sacred Collar, it still was an up and down movable object in its own right.

4. The Music Box – this object was placed on top of the Sacred Urn and when the lever was pulled downward, it made humming sounds until its last high-pitched note ended the sacred flushing waters activity.

5. The Ceremonial Burial Cap – this object was worn after the body was placed into the sarcophagus which was next to the Sacred Urn.

6. The Sacred Pendant – this item was found lodged on accident in a round hole at one end of the sarcophagus. The pendant's rubber-type substance was also found attached to a long silver-colored metal beaded chain.

7. Musical Instruments – coated in a silver metal substance, they hung from out of the wall and served two purposes: to shower the sacred

sarcophagus with holy water and make sounds
while performing this action.

*W*asn't that fun? Thanks to David Macaulay's
clever parody, *Motel of the Mysteries.*
Even Howard Carson's name was a play on the name
Howard Carter, a British archaeologist, who discovered the
steps leading to the tomb of King Tutankhamen in Egypt's
Valley of the Kings in 1922. But Carter was a professional
excavator and knew what he was doing. Carson fumbled his
way through. Carter carefully explored the four-room tomb
over several years, uncovering an incredible collection of
several thousand objects found miraculously intact. With
extensive knowledge, Carter and his other paleontologists
knew what they were finding. Carson, of course, could
only guess.

Oglethorpe University in Atlanta, Georgia is not leaving
future generations to surmise what they contributed to their
time capsule. More than half a century ago, an extraordinary
vault was designed to store records for more than six thousand years. The Oglethorpe Atlanta Crypt of Civilization, a
tomb of epic scale, was "the first successful attempt to bury a
record for any future inhabitants."

Struck by the lack of information on ancient civilizations
while teaching and researching, Oglethorpe's president,
Thornwell Jacobs, explained at length an idea to *Scientific
American* magazine for preserving contemporary records
about the year 1936 for posterity. He planned a future exhibition of customs, manner of life, and accumulated knowledge
of mankind up until that time. His plan was to preserve

consciously for the first time in history a thorough record of civilization, which he called a "crypt."

The distant date of 8113 A.D. was proposed for the opening. It was calculated by the first fixed date in history, 4241 B.C., when, most historians agreed, the Egyptian calendar was established. Exactly 6177 years had passed between 4241 B.C. and 1936 A.D., and Oglethorpe's president projected the same period of time forward from 1936, which made the crypt's opening date to be 8113 A.D.

Before suggestions of everyday life in 1936 would be added, the time capsule had to be built. A room on campus containing a swimming pool, twenty feet long, ten feet wide, and ten feet high, and whose foundation was already impervious to water, was remodeled. "The floor was raised with concrete with a heavy layer of damp proofing applied. The gallery's extended granite walls were lined with vitreous porcelain enamel embedded in pitch. The tomb had a two-foot thick stone floor and a stone roof seven feet thick. Jacobs consulted the Bureau of Standards in Washington for technical advice for storing the contents of the mausoleum. Inside would be sealed stainless steel receptacles with glass linings, filled with the inert gas of nitrogen to prevent oxidation or the aging process. A stainless steel door would seal the crypt. The entire chamber lay on bedrock Appalachian granite in the foundation of Phoebe Hearst Memorial Hall, a collegiate Gothic granite building which Jacobs optimistically reckoned would stand for 'two to five thousand years.'"

By 1937, Oglethorpe's time capsule had been featured in *Time* magazine, *Reader's Digest*, Walter Winchell's radio column, and in newspapers from Australia to London.

"On an NBC nationwide broadcast, Jacobs related that he had been struck by 'the intelligent and sympathetic reception to the plan on the part of the general public.' Articles on the crypt in the *New York Times* caught the attention of Thomas Kimmwood Peters (1884-1973), an inventor and photographer of versatile experience. Peters had been the only newsreel photographer to film the San Francisco earthquake of 1906. He had worked at Karnak and Luxor. Peters was also the inventor of the first microfilm camera using 35 millimeter film to photograph documents. In 1937, Jacobs appointed Peters as archivist of the crypt. Check out these excerpts from Oglethorpe's detailed history on the crypt to get a better idea of it:

"Jacobs and Peters combined efforts to secure the huge stainless steel door, the only outward salient symbol of the Crypt of Civilization. The American Rolling Mill in Middleton, Ohio, furnished the stainless steel for a plaque and the door. Oglethorpe University extended to David Sarnoff, president of the Radio Corporation of America, an invitation to dedicate the door on May 28, 1938. This caused considerable excitement in Atlanta, and Sarnoff s dedicatory address was broadcast on Atlanta's WSB. The setting was an open air ceremony on the Oglethorpe campus where the great stainless steel door, veiled by a huge American flag, was the centerpiece. Paramount newsreels filmed the ceremony and anticipation remained high for the crypt's sealing two years later.

"From 1937 to 1940, Peters and a staff of student assistants conducted an ambitious microfilming project. The cellulose acetate base film would be placed in hermetically sealed receptacles. Peters believed, based on the Bureau of Standards testing, that the scientifically stored film would last for six centuries; he took however, as a method of precaution, a duplicate metal film, thin as paper. Inside the crypt are microfilms of the greatest classics, including the Bible, the Koran, *The Iliad*, and Dante's *Inferno*. Producer David O. Selznick donated an original copy of the script of *Gone With The Wind*.

There are more than 640,000 pages of microfilm from over eight hundred works on the arts and sciences. Peters also used similar methods for capturing and for storing still and motion pictures. Voice recordings of political leaders such as Hitler, Stalin, Mussolini, Chamberlain, and Roosevelt were included, as were voice recordings of Popeye the Sailor and a champion hog caller. To view and to hear these pictures and sound records, Peters placed in the vault electric machines, microreaders, and projectors. In the event that electricity would not be in use in 8113 A.D., there is in the crypt a generator operated by a windmill to drive the apparatus as well as a seven power magnifier to read the microbook records by hand. The first item one would see upon entering the chamber is a thoughtful precaution: a machine to teach the English language so that the works would be more readily decipherable if found by people of a strange tongue.

"Thornwell Jacobs envisioned the crypt as a synoptic compilation and thus aimed for a whole 'museum' of not only accumulated formal knowledge of over six thousand years, but also 1930s popular culture. The list of items in the crypt is seemingly endless. All of the items were donated, with contributors as diverse as King Gustav V of Sweden and the Eastman Kodak Company. Some of the more curious items Peters included in the tomb were plastic toys—a Donald Duck, the Lone Ranger, and a Negro doll, as well as a set of Lincoln Logs. Peters also arranged with Anheuser Busch for a specially sealed ampule of Budweiser beer. The chamber of the crypt when finally finished in the spring of 1940, resembled a cell of an Egyptian pyramid, cluttered with artifacts on shelves and on the floor.

"The long awaited ceremony for the sealing of the chamber was broadcast by Atlanta's WSB radio on May 25, 1940. Some of the notables present were Ivan Allen, Dr.

Amos Ettinger, Dr. M. D. Collins, Mayor William B. Harts-
field, Clark Howell, Governor Eurith D. Rivers, and Post-
master General James A. Farley. Some of the guests gave
short messages that were preserved for the Crypt of Civilization. The impressive ceremony was darkened considerably by
the shadow of European military strife. Speaking to the
people of 8113 A.D. Dr. Jacobs said, 'The world is engaged
in burying our civilization forever, and here in this crypt, we
leave it to you.' Among the last objects to go into the vault
were records of the ceremony and a steel plate from the
Atlanta Journal, where themes of war predominated. The
great door of stainless steel was then swung into position on
its frame, where it was welded for a future that is uncertain."

When Oglethorpe University celebrated the fiftieth
anniversary of the Crypt of Civilization in the spring of 1990,
various news organizations such as the Associated Press,
NBC, ABC, CNN, National Public Radio, the *Atlanta Journal-Constitution*, the *New York Times*, and other publications
paid homage. The stationary crypt will, in some way as long
as there is hope and memory, continue to move through time
seeking to fulfill, in the words of Thornwell Jacobs, "our
archaeological duty."

But the main reason for the archaeologist parody and the
history of the Oglethorpe crypt was to get your attention to
tell you this: In that microfilm preserved and restored for the
eighty-second century is a video recording of a baseball game
played at Oglethorpe. Since baseball was America's pastime,
especially in the 1930s, a sample game was definitely
included in the crypt. In that film was a scholar-athlete, later
Chicago Cubs draftee, and left-handed pitcher on the mound
who I happened to call Daddy.

Do Not Call Me.
I'll Call You.

Our lake-friend had a cute story she shared with me not long ago. It derived from her becoming a grandmother, twice, in rather rapid succession. Her daughter and her son had babies just a few months apart. I think that's grand. They will have first cousins close to their age.

Do you know this nursery rhyme?

Monday's child is fair of face,
Tuesday's child is full of grace,
Wednesday's child is full of woe,
Thursday's child has far to go,
Friday's child is loving and giving,
Saturday's child works hard for his living,
And the child that is born on the Sabbath day
Is bonny and blithe, and good and gay.

This traditional nursery rhyme's lyrics and words were first recorded, presumably, in A.E. Bray's *Traditions of Devonshire*, volume two in 1838. The poem was used to introduce a child to the order and the different days of the week. The wording in this poem guaranteed a child would take a keen interest in which day of the week they were born on and to carry on the tradition of fortune telling by days of birth which had circulated in Suffolk since the 1570s. Sunday was traditionally referred to as the Sabbath day in Christianity. Very lovely rhyme if you were not born on a Wednesday.

I was born on a Sunday. My husband was born on a Friday. The Heir was born on a Tuesday. The Spare was born on a Saturday. If you do not know which day of the week you were born, you can find out quickly in a Google search.

Our lake-friend laughed when she mentioned the exciting news of her new grandbabies being born so close together, because it was almost a repeat of a story her mother told. Her mother was experiencing almost the same scenario. She, too, had two children who were expecting babies around the same time. And when one of her children called on a Thursday morning to announce her grandchild's arrival, she was totally awestruck. Such wonderful news! Grandbaby #1 arrived safely and mother and baby were well.

The next Thursday morning, she received another phone call. Again, marvelous news and more excitement over the arrival of grandchild #2! Our friend's mother was pleased with her children delivering healthy and happy newborns. There was not a better gift than to have everyone doing well and the thought of the new additions to her family.

But this was enough excitement for this grandmother. She said, "Loved getting all this tremendous news these past two weeks, but if anyone calls me *next* Thursday, I am *not* answering the phone!"

Bobcats, and Cougars, and Bears.
Oh, My!

*N*ot to mention armadillos, fox, deer, coyotes, birds, and our various normal house pets. We've got a regular nature preserve over here, or petting zoo—pet at your own risk.

My neighborhood has been in the news lately because of a black bear sighting. The Wildlife Resources Division hasn't found such, as yet. But I can tell you for certain, I *know* there was a bobcat. He was in my backyard about a month ago around 6:15 a.m. I heard this screeching noise and awoke from one of my few sleeping-through-the-night chances. I walked outside thinking it was a screech owl. The shriek was heard first on the right side of my wooded backyard, then middle, and then moved to the left all within about five minutes. Because of foliage from the trees and bushes, I did not see anything that early in the morning. But I heard it.

My youngest son was visiting and came outside to join me. He also heard the sound. He thought it was a bobcat. Sure enough, he researched it and listened to an audio clip of what sound a bobcat makes, and without a doubt, that's what we heard. I Googled the sound a screech owl makes. Guess what? Screech owls don't screech. What the…?

One early morning while walking her dog, my neighbor swears she saw a cougar. I can't dispute her. She's a close friend. But really? Let's describe a cougar for minute. As adults, its height is two to three feet with the male weighing 120-220 pounds and the female weighing 64-140 pounds. They are tawny brown in color and have a long tail.

My friend's across-the-street neighbor has two Rhodesian Ridgebacks secured by an electric fence. Let's compare. The Ridgeback doesn't usually bark. The cougar did not bark or growl. The Ridgeback is athletically built, as is the cougar. The dog is of the same height as the cat and, if female, the same weight. The breed is dignified and reserved with strangers, hence no need for her hollering for help when she first saw the big kitty. Ridgebacks are confident, and I'd say so are cougars. Both are brown, short-haired animals with long tails. I'm just saying. Could it be? But don't tell her I doubted that she saw a mountain lion in Newnan. I heard a bobcat, so who am I to judge?

Black bear? Well, that's different. One could have visited from Mississippi. You know that Ole Miss changed their official mascot from Colonel Reb, looking like Colonel Sanders, to the Rebel Black Bear in 2010. The state is home to two types of black bears, the American black bear and the Louisiana black bear. I don't know which one was seen here and spotted by my neighbors in their cars, thank goodness. Around lunchtime, it walked along the side of my house, crossed the street in front of my home, and joined a tree-lined sidewalk, then continued on toward the tennis courts, pool, clubhouse, and lake until out of sight. Pretty courageous, I would say. Oh, and when seen, it was trash pick-up day. Now we know what lured him.

To this day, the Wildlife Resources Division has no surveillance. But I am telling you, like in the movie *Poltergeist*, when the little blonde daughter turned to her parents and said, "They're here," they are.

Microeconomics
101

I wasted this great lesson plan on a room full of sixth graders. Or did I? It wasn't a waste, really, except sixth graders don't remember much about middle school. And this lesson was an important one. I was conducting an economic exercise.

I took a break from teaching before our second baby was born and sold real estate for John Wieland Developments, a large and successful real estate company primarily in metro Atlanta. Since 1970, he has built neighborhood friendly homes around clubhouses, Olympic size swimming pools for swim meets but also with slides for the kiddies, nature trails, lakes, golf courses, and such to offer something for everyone. His business has/had its own lumber, real estate, interior design, and financing companies under one roof. He sold houses like car dealers sell cars: choose a house plan, then for a pre-set price you can have more, like four-sided brick homes, or a garden tub, maybe a screen porch, or that sunroom. Just tack it on to the base price of the house. Every purchaser is really not so individualistic after all. It's pre-arranged. You can get extra on that base plan, if you pay for it.

What was the point I was making? A *real-life wake-up-call*.

Remember *Parade* magazine, which was an insert to the *Atlanta Journal-Constitution* newspaper? Every year they featured in this supplement "What People Earn." On that yearly cover, tiny little portraits of about one hundred people from every walk of life were featured with their occupation and income. I cut out those pictures, placed males' images in one envelope and females' in another. There were incomes ranging from under $10,000 to over a million. People in the service industry, teachers, postal workers, professional football players, models, car salesmen, dentists…you name it. A variety of people from different ages, backgrounds, colors, and education were all featured.

The male students picked a random person from the male envelope and the females from theirs. Because I kept my John Wieland Development's Collection of house plans, I began my lesson by using one of his designs: "Here's an average house. And its cost to build on an average lot is [fill in the blank]." I described down payment, private mortgage insurance, home owner's insurance, utilities, etc. I mentioned if they bought a car what monthly payments might be for that also, and I mentioned possible grocery costs.

Then, after explaining what all was involved with debt, I randomly picked students to reveal their income from the people they chose from the envelopes. Could they afford this basic home? Most could. Then I placed a carrot in front of them, which was another house, but this one had all the bells and whistles.

"Hey, look! I want that garden tub in my house," some would say.

"You can't afford it," I answered to several. "But those with the large incomes can."

"Why are some getting a screened-in porch and I'm not? I want that screen porch!" a few more interjected.

I mentioned, "You can't get it. Not with your down payment. If you want to put more down, banks might lower your mortgage. Unless you've saved enough, you won't be able to change the numbers on that."

"But I want it!"

"Yeah, well, maybe if you were married. A dual income changes everything. You probably could afford it then."

Wait a minute. I could see the light bulbs go off in their twelve-year-old heads!

And then the scrambling started. Boys were chasing the most financially successful girls and girls were trying to catch the most prosperous boys. All over the classroom you heard, "Will you marry me?"

And now the other lesson learned was that these pretend professionals who had either advanced degrees or somehow worked hard toward an end goal of comfortable wealth realized they didn't need a partner. Male and female students, because of the luck of the draw in their chosen person, actually realized the importance of being profitable enough and what it brought to the playing field. They could do it alone if they wanted. They had a choice.

I do hope their adolescent brains retained something from this.

Sometimes I Give Myself
the Creeps

*D*o you ever feel that way?

I have the gift and the curse of gab. It has gotten me in and out of trouble more times than I care to admit. It has opened doors and closed doors. I have gained friends and I have lost friends. It is entertaining, some have said, and yet overbearing, said others. It has put people at ease and yet worn people out. I have laughed at my own cleverness but sometimes I can't stand myself.

There are very few people who know how to take me. One was my dear friend Nannoo. Before she died, we were running buddies; with our third amigo, we three single women in our early twenties were seen everywhere together in Atlanta. If only two of us were coupled without the third for some reason, and since we three looked rather similar, people would confuse us and not recognize the correct two standing in front of them. I was called, by mistake, Nannoo or our third amigo many times. It really didn't matter.

After attending a home football game at the University of Georgia in Athens one fall Saturday afternoon in the early 1980s, we were left stranded because we had no idea what we had done with our dates when the game was over. Either we unknowingly ditched them or they ditched us. We saw some Atlanta buddies at the Kappa Alpha frat lawn party, the place to see and be seen before and after football games.

They offered us a ride back from Athens, and while driving home, it began to get dark and it also began to rain. All four of us were in this teeny tiny Volkswagen Beetle with the boys in the front and the girls in the back. Nannoo started yakking about all the events that had taken place. Before there were iPhone updates and texting like we have today to keep up with the latest gossip, this was now our time to catch up with our selected and inebriated memories from earlier in the day.

Nannoo's laugh was a cackle…loud and ear-piercing. We laughed until we cried at our own stories and each other's. I am sure the alcohol-induced dialogue made it funnier. Or, at least we thought so. The boys were trapped in the front seat while one was trying to steer and the other was trying to help navigate, at night, in the downpour. The rain pounded on our driver's little car and we were the "stereo" in the backseat turned up full force. It was driving them crazy trying to keep their composure to safely get us home, which was more than an hour away, while what sounded more like hail than water droplets continued to beat down on us in the dark on the two-lane road from Athens to Atlanta.

Finally, the guy sitting in shotgun couldn't take it anymore and turned around and waved his hands in front of our faces and said, "Shut up! You both are talking so loud and so fast that I don't see how you both can understand what the other is saying!"

Without missing a beat, Nannoo replied, "Well, Lee can listen as fast as I can talk."

I am not sure we saw those guys again back in our stomping ground for a while. I knew then I was a menace at times…so much so that I occasionally took inventory of myself.

I followed the George Costanza rule of "go out on a high note." In episode sixteen of season nine, entitled *The Burning*, George landed a one-two punch with a good idea followed by verbal zinger in a meeting with his associates at

Kruger Industries. Kruger was the dimwitted owner of the company, and when George told a great joke in front him and his colleagues, he was surprised at the tremendous reaction from it. His thought process was, "Get out while the gettin's good." Instead of falling flat on your face in a bald attempt to maintain, leave on a high note. Leave while all of your co-workers are in awe and wanting more.

And that is why when I get sick of myself and think others might feel the same, I just stay out of everyone else's hair.

While teaching school, my English department was assigned the same lunch time every day. They wanted us to visit, get to know each other better and bond, hopefully talk shop, and learn from each other in that measly thirty minutes they called lunch. We no longer had to watch and monitor the students during that time; there were other supervisors for that. We could enjoy adult time. But the cafeteria was pretty far away from our rooms, and walking there, breaking in line in front of the kids—sorry—and getting back to our quiet table in a teacher's classroom now only left us about twenty minutes to gobble down our food and discuss classroom or literature matters.

That's where my gift/curse could take over, and I thoughtfully and respectfully did not join the round of teachers every day of every week. I gave them a gift, and that was to not have to deal with me all the time during lunch. I would rather have had them ask me, "Where were you at lunch today? We missed you," than think, or, in my horror, say to someone else, "I sure am glad Lee didn't show up today. She talks all the time."

I was thinking like George: "Quit while you are ahead. Always leave them wanting more."

The Family
Jewels

*Y*eah, you know what I am talking about, right? So, if you don't want to read this, skip it. But it's rated PG.

Around the age of eight, we were leaving it to our oldest son to become more independent in his cleanliness routines: teeth, hair, manhood, and other body parts. We felt like we didn't have to check up on him anymore, except on rare occasions, of which this is one.

Playing in a late recreation basketball game one school night, we had to dash home to go through that routine and get to bed at a decent time. Once the habitual businesses were finished for the evening, and thinking he might have skimped on some because of being hurried to beat the clock for bedtime, I started pumping questions, "Did you wash your hair?" He answered, "Yes." "Did you brush your teeth?" And again. he answered, "Yes." But most importantly, "Did you clean your teapot?"

Okay, we called it a teapot. Not having brothers who might have given it another name, my husband's parents named it and, therefore, we carried on the family tradition. My high school boyfriend's parents called it a tack hammer. Saying the actual name of the thing is awful and utterly ridiculous. As a civil society, how did we adopt such grotesque names for our private parts?

He finally answered in the affirmative.

"Let me see," I responded.

Snooping around his pearly whites. Check.

A smell and glance at his shampooed hair. Check.

A quick peek of his underarms. Check.

And then down below—*Oh! No!*

Both of my boys were big babies. This child weighed in at nine pounds, three ounces. His younger brother later beat him by an ounce. They stayed in the 97% at the doctor's office on the weight and height checks during all their pediatrician-checkup lives. They grew into six-foot-one-inch and six-foot-six-inch men. Everything about them was advanced in the growth department. But at the age of eight, who would have thought this? I was dumbfounded. This child was still in elementary school and what I was thinking must have passed my lips because I said, "You've got pubic hair!"

"What's that?" he asked.

Oh no, I really did exclaim that thought openly and now I've got to explain it.

Collecting my emotions and trying to respond in textbook jargon only the biological definition, I said matter-of-factly that pubic hair was "the protective covering of the genitalia...blah, blah, blah...something-else-I-didn't-remember-but-trying-not-to-sound-like-a-distraught-mother." I instructed him to go see his father in the other room and show him. While observing our newfound discovery, I heard Hubby expounding on our son's developing body. I heard words like, "growing up," "becoming a man," "this is what happens as you get older," etc.

Then I heard, "What did your mother say?"

The Heir said, "Oh, she's in the other room crying."

Wouldn't you be if your eight-year-old was already becoming a man?

When the little brother came along, typical sibling behaviors started—I wouldn't know but have been told. There was punching, kicking, pushing...over little things. The Spare, while growing up under the influences of an older brother and more knowledgeable because of it, made me nervous while he played with his only-children friends because of what he might introduce to them.

One sweet little friend's younger sister hadn't been born yet and while these two played together, I kept a watchful eye and listening ear out for what mine might introduce to this innocent. I learned a good bit of information early on because of my girlfriend who had an older sister and she was only *two* years older. I was about nine when she told me where babies come from. *Not my parents*, I thought.

With my boys being eight years apart, it was terrifying to me that my oldest was going to be the one who might eventually spill the beans to the youngest about Santa, the Easter Bunny, or The Tooth Fairy. I don't think my baby, at four, heard about that yet from his twelve-year-old brother, but I bet he only had a few more years of innocence.

One day after a play date, our youngest and I were in the car driving his friend home. The Spare chose then and there to inform me that his older brother had, "kicked him in the nuts."

Uh-oh. There it was, an honest statement about brotherly roughhousing using our family name for the male genitalia. Now what? Before he could explain the situation, his friend, overhearing his statement, piped up and asked, "What are nuts?"

Well, thank goodness I interrupted before my youngest started to explain. I shuddered to think how my preschooler was going to answer that one. I didn't want that sweet buddy of his to learn about that from *my* child. So I turned my head quickly, my eyes penetrating his, and started shaking it, demonstrating the meaning, "No. Don't you go there. No, sir.

Don't you say a word!" He figured out what he wasn't supposed to do and I changed the subject.

That was the last thing I wanted that virtuous young'un to have on his mind and on the tip of his tongue before he met his mother when we dropped him off. Can you imagine him asking her about what being "kicked in the nuts" meant?

Let me leave you with this thought. Stop reading now if you aren't prepared for this upcoming PG-13 anecdote. Here is a quote I find funny. And it would even be funnier if Betty White really had said it. But I think it's misattributed. It does seem something like Sue Ann Nivens, her character on *The Mary Tyler Moore Show*, might say. In playing Sue Ann, Betty White played up her character as a cheerful, home-and-hearth loving woman who was the host of her own Minneapolis, Minnesota fictional WJM-TV show, *The Happy Homemaker*. Her program delivered advice to housewives on decorating and cooking. She chose unusual and sometimes ludicrous themes for some episodes, such as "What's all this fuss about famine?" and "A salute to fruit."

As tame and sweet as Sue Ann appeared, behind her domesticated show's camera was a backbiting, sardonic, and sexually voracious woman. And Betty White played Sue Ann perfectly, with honesty and derogatory wit. So it's plausible that Betty—I mean, Sue Ann might have said, "Why do people say, 'grow some balls'? Balls are weak and sensitive. If you wanna be tough, grow a vagina. Those things can take a pounding."

And she didn't use nicknames for those body parts, either.

The Purloined
Letter?

I saw *Murder on the Orient Express* recently. This 2017 mystery/drama/comedy, adapted from Agatha Christie's book of the same title, has been produced many times. So many that Christie's world-renowned detective, Hercule Poirot, has been played by twenty-one actors, some of whom you might recognize over the decades: Charles Laughton, Orson Welles, Jose Ferrer, Tony Randall, Albert Finney, Peter Ustinov, Ian Holm, John Moffatt, Alfred Molina, and this year, Kenneth Branagh.

The film is in the fourth adaptation of her novel and the storyline reveals that this acclaimed detective seeks to solve a murder on the famous European train in the 1930s. Poirot is a Belgian former police officer, now a private investigator. Christie's inspiration for his creation was the stories by Sir Arthur Conan Doyle. In *An Autobiography*, Christie states, "I was still writing in the Sherlock Holmes tradition, eccentric detective, stooge assistant, with an Inspector-Lestrade-type Scotland Yard detective..." For his part, Conan Doyle acknowledged basing his detective stories on the model of Edgar Allan Poe's sleuth.

Poe's *The Purloined Letter* is an American short story and the third of his three detective stories featuring the fictional C. Auguste Dupin. These stories of 1844 are considered to be important early forerunners of the modern detective story. Do you like mysteries? I do, and my mother needed a private eye to figure out a letter she received from my father during WWII. Let's see if you can solve her dilemma.

Here are the facts:

1. Woman (my mother) works in her small town as a teacher. Her husband (my father) is in the Navy on a destroyer outside of Italy during WWII.
2. Only form of communication between them is letter writing.
3. Mail is not fast communication.
4. They write letters religiously back and forth.
5. My father could not relay information in his letters about his naval activities or his locations because of the tempestuous war situation.
6. The war office read the letters being sent back home to the United States to make sure the correspondence from the young service men did not carry any information in them which could be intercepted and used against our country in the war if intercepted by the enemy.
7. There was a saying at that time, "Loose lips sink ships."
8. Mother received a letter from Father that started in the normal way, "Dear Darling."
9. The entire body/middle part of the letter was totally cut out.
10. The letter was signed, "Your Loving Husband."
11. In other words, Mother received a mailed document with a rectangle-shaped cut-out in the middle.
12. Mother asked herself, "What did he say? Did he write secrets that should not have been revealed? Will he get into trouble if so?"
13. My worried mother wrote back to my father to determine what happened.

14. Weeks passed.
15. In the next letter, he relinquished the secret of the letter's missing body content.

What do you think happened?

Read below for answer. Words are written backwards. You must decipher it, because, after all, it is a mystery.

In Mother's own words:

"siH rewsna tuoba eht suoiverp tuo-tuc rettel saw taht eh dewo em a rettel, saw oot derit ot etirw, dna detnaw tsuj ot tel em wonk eh saw evila"

Good luck with that cryptic message.

P.S. My daddy—that prankster!

Let me help you get started. It begins, "His answer about the previous cut-out letter…"

Testing, *Testing*

Winter break is over and students have settled into their school routine once again. The county school calendar is divided into two semesters of eighteen weeks each. With one semester down, ending before Christmas, this second semester is about half over. That means there are only about nine more weeks left until summer. Just nine weeks! This doesn't include spring break in April.

And here at the midpoint of the second semester, testing is not uncommon. No one looks forward to tests—students, because they have to take them, or teachers, because they have to grade them. Being an English teacher is not easy when it comes to grading. Essays, remember? I used to jokingly say while grading and drinking wine, "I wonder if the more I drink, the better they'll do."

Another hardship on an English teacher during the year, and especially at midterm testing, was the copying machine that would break down at the most inopportune time. And it just didn't break down for an hour. Sometimes it was days. Somebody had to call the company to send someone out to fix it. And by fix it, I mean that took all day, too. One couldn't wait to see the taped sign that said, *NOT WORKING!* taken off the top of the machine. By the time it was removed, there was mold on it.

Before the copier, we used the mimeograph machine— often abbreviated to mimeo—and it was a low-cost duplicating machine that worked by forcing ink through a stencil onto paper. I loved that smell of that ink running through the machine. Not for long lengths of time, though. I heard one could get high from the smell by the overuse of the machine.

Did I mention bathroom duty? My pre-twenty-first century schools had us rotate bathroom duty assignments. I could never, *ever* eat my lunch in the girls' bathroom during duty time like one teacher I know who did. She scooted a desk in there and plopped her lunch tray on top of it and dug in to that cafeteria mystery meat, cold mashed potatoes, green peas, apple sauce, and milk. This lunch probably only cost the teacher $1.25 in the 1970s, but I am sure she would have gladly paid for something more appropriate to her tastes if it were offered. Finally, a teacher menu did catch on, a little higher in price, but one could still eat the student lunch as a choice. They even had a salad bar just for teachers as well. And there was even tea at the teacher's table. Woohoo!

One of my teacher girlfriends left public school education and was hired at Atlanta's prestigious Westminster School, a very exclusive private school. She and I kept up with each other and she would report to me that she did still have high school bus and bathroom duty but that it wasn't for the obvious reasons of keeping order—it was because they didn't want any of their students with the million-dollar last names kidnapped from that pricey school.

Do You Pass
Muster?

I've lived in Georgia all my life. Except for second and third homes at a lake in Alabama and at a beach in Florida, my primary residence has always been Georgia. Lately, though, when you visit and stay long enough, learn where to grocery shop, meet neighbors, join groups, plan activities around your new dwelling, it takes up a place in your heart.

But nothing can claim the sixty-four years of being a Georgian; I like people and want to establish intimacy sooner, rather than later. My family on both sides, maternal and paternal, are several generations of living in Georgia. Reunions, family gatherings, raising children in the church your parents were married in and that your children were baptized in, with second, third, and fourth cousins in the audience, is a big deal to me. I am an only child. Because I didn't want to wait so long for establishing a new friendship at my lake, beach, or the new town we eventually left my clan for, I thought, how could I get to know a person quickly and feel like we had been life-long friends?

So, to get to know a person quicker, I decided if I could find out the answers to just three questions with the theme being the same, just asked in a different manner but where all the answers would be identical, then, by golly, I'd have some established new friends. I developed my questionnaire. I didn't want to wait years to get to know someone in my new dwellings. I was fifty when I came up with this survey. I wanted to develop deep friendships instantly. Who was more like me, thought like me, and could especially take me for periods at a time? You know, who was my type of crazy?

All answers were general and stereotypical.

Question One: Do/Did you live with boys?

Boys are generally messy. I know. I have two. They dropped their trousers around the house everywhere they went. They were smelly. Boys just had a mind of their own that girls really didn't get at times and sometimes they would forget their manners. They were unclean—that means their personal habits could be annoying. Teachers tended to prefer girls—who were cleaner—instead of those stinky boys in middle school. Like bulls in a china shop, boys are rough, scruffy, gangly, and broke things because they were clumsy. They peed and missed/dripped at their destination. But even with this bad behavior you loved them anyway. Therefore, any new friend of mine had to understand boys' ways. They made your life crazy! If you have boys and I have boys, let's go through this circus called life together.

Question Two: Do/Did you live with dogs?

Dogs are generally messy. I know. I've had several. They were smelly. Dogs had a mind of their own sometimes if they were not trained right, and even then, a squirrel or chipmunk caused them to forget their manners. They were dirty most times from getting into things they shouldn't, which would be annoying. I preferred girl dogs instead of boy dogs because at least if a girl unexpectedly peed, it was in one location instead of two—chair leg and carpet—like boy dogs. Big dogs have big wagging tails and are clumsy like bulls in a china shop. Dogs sometimes threw up gross stuff and defecated at the most inconvenient times, like when you had company. But even with this bad behavior you loved them anyway. Therefore, this second question is like the first and any new friend of mine had to understand dogs' ways. They made your life crazy! If you have dogs and I have dogs, let's you and I, and maybe our dogs, make a play date.

Question Three: Do/Did you consume alcohol?

People who overindulge in alcohol may become messy. I know several. They think they do not smell of alcohol and can fool you into thinking they are not overserved, but they are fooling no one. They also have a drunken mind of their own since they also think they are the most clever and smartest person in the room, but mostly they converse annoyingly. They start to look unshapely over the course of the drinking period. They forget their manners and share outrageous remarks or become clumsy like bulls in a china shop and break things…maybe a chair leg or the glass that held their spirits. They have to pee a lot or sometimes they even regurgitate. But even with this out of character bad behavior you loved them anyway. If you enjoy having spirits, let's go get a cocktail together and plan a mini-vacation.

Well, how did you do in this three-prong questionnaire?

See how the questions are really one and the same? And to make it easy on any new friend of mine, you only had to answer one of the three questions correctly, because guess what? It meant, with just one of the queries, that you are not an uptight person and can handle my messy character and possibly still like/love me. And I know it's telling me that we are going to fit together nicely.

P.S. If you think it will help you find new friends fast, you are welcome to use this poll for your own investigation.

"I Can't Take It *Anymore!*"

*Y*ou've heard the jokes about it. Here's one from Rita Rudner: "I love being married. It's so great to find that one special person you want to annoy for the rest of your life."

Author Ogden Nash once said, "Marriage is the bond between a person who never remembers anniversaries and another who never forgets them." Let's face it, marriage is hard work. When Hubby and I were getting married and it was mandatory for us to attend pre-wedding counseling with our minister, he commented, "Marriage is in the trenches." He was right. It takes hard work to overlook the failures you find in each other over the years: the physical tics/behaviors the other possesses that disturb you, the physical noises that the other donates that exasperate you, and so on. But being annoyed with your spouse didn't happen overnight.

"Marriage is a wonderful institution…but who wants to live in an institution?" said Groucho Marx.

Sometimes you might feel like you are in one. You know everything about your partner and then some after decades of marriage

My girlfriend, Tie-one-ona, was married for twenty-five years when she was realized she and her husband had crossed over from bliss to reality. It hadn't happened overnight. But there they were. And like many couples after decades of marriage, complacency and bad habits set in. Her plight is not unusual. Now empty nesters, they were enjoying each other with no demands of a child being at home. It was their turn to enjoy their life without another human being's contention. It was all about each other. Did you read that? *All about each other*…every single day…and every hour…and every second. Just them. Day in. Day out. Just the two of them…at home…alone.

Able to reconnect with their shared interests, one of those was watching their favorite television shows together. This intimacy was a special time. They'd have an early dinner at around 5:00 p.m., clean up the kitchen, Tie would get a scoop of her favorite ice cream, her husband his favorite beer, and then find a show that interested them both. They started binge-watching *Breaking Bad*. Getting comfortable and watching this drama together sometimes kept them up until one or two in the morning. Having pre-recorded the series, they might look at each other after one or two episodes' cliffhangers and say, "Got another in ya?" and go for it.

But sometimes, while she was out of town for work, her mate would sneak in ahead of her and watch an episode they planned to watch together when she returned. He never mentioned he had but sometimes she could tell because…he fell asleep.

Because of the beer, because he was tired, because he had previously watched that episode, and because it was getting really late, he sometimes dozed off. And when he did, he snored. She didn't mind his previous viewing but she did mind the snoring. He didn't snore in bed. Why now? Although he was on the couch and she was in *her* recliner, the sounds he was making while sleeping interrupted her being able to hear the dialogue. She told me she could live for days in that recliner as she had everything she needed at her fingertips on the table next to her—bottled water, crackers, Q-tips, Kleenex, magazines, TV remote, etc. She shared that she tried everything to wake him without having to get out of her comfy seat...she clapped her hands, she whistled, she called his name, she snapped her fingers, and she threw every little thing she had at her disposal at him from that table to get his attention, but he didn't budge and continued snoring. Nothing, *nothing*, she tried worked.

Seeing his cell phone in his lap, she called his number, and when it rang, the snoring ended. Stupefied, he first looked at whose name was on the screen of the incoming call. Not having his glasses on, he was befuddled as to whose name was on the caller identification, but he answered anyway with a groggy, "Whello?"

"Stop," came the reply on the other end.

Not fully awake and perplexed, he replied, "Huh? Whatszat?"

"Stop snoring."

Spoiled
Rotten

Because my parents were forty before I, an only child, arrived, my mother spoiled my father. She really pampered Daddy. He, in turn, learned to keep the toilet seat down after its use. That is L-O-V-E in my book. It was what I was used to growing up and had come to expect as normal. But the boys in my house—all of them—never did that for me. I am sure once or twice during a middle-of-the-night lavatory visit, I fell in because there was no lid-protection. Thank you very much!

But even while the toilet seat continued to stay up, I indulged my boys. I must have that spoiled-rotten-DNA-gene, too. When I made lasagna for my family, one fourth was created for The Spare, who liked his meal as though he was ordering a meat-lovers pizza—nothing but pasta, sauce, and meat. The more meat the better, just hold the onions and mushrooms. My portion was meatless but made with oodles of onions, mushrooms, and cheese. Hubby and The Heir liked everything in theirs, but whereas Hubby liked even amounts of all the ingredients, The Heir liked less onions and mushrooms in his quarter section. One lasagna constructed in fourths. It was trouble doing that but it was sprinkled with a dash of love.

Mother pampered me like that, too. Sometimes while running errands, she brought home girlish goodies. Spoiling me like this for no reason, people around town made comments to her about it, and she responded, "It's just showing lots of love." The only disappointments I remember when she came home without any presents were my highest requests…a baby brother or sister. Hadn't she gone to visit someone in the hospital where those babies were lined up behind the window just for the picking? Didn't you check them out like library books? That's what I thought when I was little. Each time she left to see someone at the hospital, I *always* pleaded, "Please bring home a baby brother or sister." She consistently answered, "I'll try." Of course, she'd come through the door empty-handed.

When my parents retired, my mother really wanted to travel. Daddy had already been places with his professional baseball career and being on a destroyer during WWII. But mother had not been to such interesting places and now they had the time and the money. Daddy told us to go without him. He felt like he had seen enough. We did. Our first excursion was to Hawaii and San Francisco in 1977. Leaving Daddy alone for twelve days, she made sure he was taken care of by planning and cooking twelve different dinners to enjoy while we were gone. Although the Amana Corporation introduced the countertop microwave oven in 1967, we didn't have one.

Not only did my mother cook the dinners, she wrapped them in aluminum foil, labeled for each day of the week we were gone, and placed the dozen in the freezer so all Daddy had to do was take one out, lay it on the counter to thaw, and warm it up for that night's dinner. With only the Dairy Queen available for fast food, this solved her worry about what he would do for his meals while we were gone. She knew he could fend for himself at lunch. Here was another example of spoiling—I mean, love.

When we returned, she found that all her energy of creating all those meals just for him was wasted. They had not been touched and were still in the freezer. Friends and family swooped in and looked after Daddy for us by taking him out to lunch and dinner every day. My helpless, spoiled Daddy, my own boys. Oh, and me...just tiny examples of being spoiled rotten.

Brain Fog –
Everyone Needs a
Mrs. Wiggins!

*W*ho remembers Mrs. Wiggins from the 1970s *Carol Burnett Show*? What a fiasco she was at her job. Yet, Mr. Tudball still needed a secretary. Having her was better than none at all.

I sometimes think we could all benefit from a personal assistant or secretary…especially those forgetful middle school or high school students. Teaching in the middle school, I had to take the course The Middle School Learner to keep my 6-12 grades teaching certificate current for five years. While teaching Gifted students and learning more about brain development because of my classes, I became convinced it might be necessary to help those who are in a fog have some kind of personal organizer.

Our county gave our students an agenda to write down due dates for assignments, but if you lost things, like most did at that age, then not losing the agenda was one of those items at the top of the list. I had an entire collection of left-behind agendas in my room at the end of the day. Believe me, I remember many excuses from even the most gifted students about why their homework wasn't turned in on time—or not at all.

"I made a cake for my cell structure project, but my parents ate it."

"I left my homework in the back of my dad's pickup truck and he drove through a car wash."

"It slipped out of my hands and blew away so I started chasing it. And that's why I am late for school."

"My dad forgot to do it for me."

The teen brain—in a quick rundown—is still under construction. A teen is much more drawn to the immediate reward of a situation than adults are. They are much less likely to think ahead and think about the future. The future can be just an hour later. And the male brain takes a long time to work its way into an adult version, which I most recently read to be—hold on to your seat—around twenty-seven to twenty-nine years old. I still have a child that is twenty-two and am holding out hope for a quicker entry into adulthood.

My family just got back from the lake, where my oldest brought along one of his best friends since middle school, and visiting with him again after not seeing him for a few years, the memories of his middle school behavior flooded back because I was also his teacher. Jay has been the topic of several of my conversations and stories over the years because he is certainly high voltage and his mind never shuts off. He is also a delight.

I fondly recall one day when he was in sixth grade. I have no idea the discussion going on in the classroom, but I do remember Jay politely raising his hand, and when called upon, he said, "Last night, when I stayed up past bedtime reading the M volume of the Encyclopedia Britannica, I noticed…" I do not recollect a thing after that preface. This brilliant student read volumes of the encyclopedia *for fun*.

We would take Jay on vacations with us during his middle school years. One time, Hubby and I enjoyed, but were surprised by, the conversation going on in the backseat of our car. It was the discussion between two thirteen-year-old boys and Jay's analysis of the different war fronts during WWII… where and what the Germans, the French, and the Americans did in their respective theaters. I mean, thirteen! And my husband turned to me and said, "He's right." I thought middle school boys might discuss fishing, video games, or heck, maybe even girls a little bit. Jay was an accurate history resource.

But he rarely turned in his homework, even when he used the school agenda for organizational help. I called his mother, a friend, and told her I had an idea. Let's get Jay a secretary. Maybe she could pay some really organized girl—I know it was stereotypical, but more of the female students I knew were advanced in organization those years—to call Jay and remind him outside of class about the assignments that were due. It would be a win-win! A middle school girl would have some extra money. Jay is reminded of what is due in school. His mother doesn't have to have a heart attack when he doesn't turn in his work and gets a *zero* in the teacher's grade book and has to have to have a parent conference with his teacher a zillion times during the school year. His mother doesn't have to be involved *at all*!

I mean, if both of my children had needed help like this, I'd have done it. Mine were just mildly forgetful—worrisome enough. But Jay was one of those genius students who, on our lake trip, thought during his visit he had lost his only pair of prescription glasses, and if he had lost them, he really could not see, and there he was leaving in a couple of weeks to work in China for a year. That would have been tough, trying to secure another pair before he left the country in that short amount of time. He also couldn't keep up with his phone the entire weekend.

And his age?

Thirty-two.

I still *love* this man/boy! But, God, please bless him in China.

I'm a KD
Lady

I am a Kappa Delta.

I used to say, "I was a Kappa Delta." I was soon corrected about that and learned that once a sorority girl, always a sorority girl.

Who would have thought being song leader for my chapter at Georgia Southern University in 1973 would prove so valuable when I started teaching Gifted ninth grade English in 2006? Since I am a tactile person, my philosophy had always been to incorporate as many of the five senses into my lesson plans to reach all the different learning styles. Maybe some new thought that I was teaching and presented in different ways would stick.

And it did.

The Odyssey, an ancient epic poem by Homer, is required reading in my county's ninth grade English curriculum. Because of the Greek setting, every year I would tell my students that I could sing the Greek alphabet. What a hidden talent. Hoping to take away from class instruction, students always begged me to sing it. Of course, I did. It was in my lesson plan repertoire, they just didn't know it. They were impressed. But the ham I am, I kept going.

Would they like to hear me sing some more Greek songs? "Of course!" they urged. "Take all the time you need until the bell rings! This is different!" Because I was affiliated with music—from piano to voice—since childhood, I remembered the Greek songs from the other sororities when I went through rush and visited their chapters:

Alpha Delta Pi sang, "Pi, Pi, ADPi, like 'em, love 'em, 'til I die…"

Zeta Tau Alpha serenaded, "Well, I'm a Zeta. Zeta. Zeta, Zeta, Z-T-A…"

Phi Mu crooned, "Phi Mu, Phi Mu, Phi Mu Fraternity, Phi Mu, Phi Mu, Phi Mu for me…"

Now I had their undivided attention.

"More! More!" they shouted.

Next, I belted out those from my Kappa Delta, "With a K, with a K, with a K-a-a, and a P, and a P, and a P-p-a, Kappa Delta!

But their favorite—and mine—was:

"I'm a KD Lady, I'm a red hot baby, I'm the hottest thing in town. And when it comes to lovin', I'm a human oven, I can burn you right down to the ground."

And with that last line, I'd lick my thumb, place it on my hip and say, "Psssst."

Now, this may have seemed like I was wasting time. But remember, "Psssst" is an onomatopoeia for those who remember their English literary terms, and this demonstrated that I could not only tie in Greek songs to my lessons, but literary terms.

I'm good.

Now they are hootin', hollerin', and clapping! They may not remember what *The Odyssey* was about but they'll never forget they studied it…somehow.

Fast forward four years. One of those precious students in that classroom was graduating from high school. She told her mother, my neighbor, that she wanted to be a Kappa Delta at the University of Georgia. I was totally excited. I wrote her a recommendation and she pledged! It was my policy to wait until my former students had graduated before friending them on Facebook. And since that class of 2010 had moved on out of the building, I could be friends with them now and keep up with their adventures in the college world.

Finding out that she was not only my darling former student but also now going to be a sorority sister, I made her a KD scrapbook so she could collect all her sorority memorabilia from her future activities that she was going to have at UGA. Her mother later told me how much she treasured it and how packed it became during her time at college.

When I learned about her pledging, I posted on Facebook that this student was going to be a KD and how proud I was. I heard back from another great student from that same graduating class who wrote on my Facebook wall, "Well, of course! She is now a KD Lady and red hot baby!"

These students were fourteen or fifteen years old when I sang that song. They were now eighteen or nineteen and that one sweet former student remembered that silly classroom moment.

I wonder if she remembers what *The Odyssey* was really about.

Acting
Presidential

*T*he president's agenda:

1. a promise to lead the people to victory in the presidential election
2. a promise to build a strong and just nation
3. a promise to eliminate poverty
4. a promise to dignify labor
5. a promise to reshape the economy

Trump? Or was it Obama?

Neither. It was Argentina's president, Juan Perón, who served from 1946 until 1955 when he was thrown out of his country.

My mother taught high school government in the 1950s. There was only one high school, therefore, only one government teacher. But because government was a required credit to graduate, like it is today, everyone had to pass through her classroom.

One of her students had eventual influence on the national level in the political arena and you may have heard his name. Many more outstanding students passed through those halls after she retired—an Oscar winner, Pulitzer Prize winner, pro athletes, and many other national success stories.

But this student sitting in her government classroom heard her give a government lesson about Juan Perón, the Argentine general and politician who was elected three times as president of Argentina. Perón was overthrown in a military coup in 1955. She mentioned in this 1959 classroom, "Mark my words. Perón will be back." This gifted young student must have taken her words to heart.

He graduated from high school and earned his B.B.A. in economics from the University of Georgia in 1964. He became an assistant professor of economics at Georgia State University. He later earned his Ph.D. in economics in 1969 from the University of Virginia. As wonderful as this career seems, his star was still rising.

This young man's name was James C. Miller, III. In July 1985, President Ronald Reagan chose this "conservative economist who favors reducing the size of the federal government" as his administration's new budget director.

Before his rise in the Reagan administration and his movement up this brilliant career ladder, he must not have forgotten his high school roots and his government teacher. When Perón returned to power in 1973, although briefly, as he only served for nine months until his death in 1974 when he was succeeded by his third wife, Eva, Jimmy wrote a letter to my mother about this event, which she kept with other cards and letters that I now have.

I am now retired myself and still wonder what kind of influence we teachers had on all our students after they became adults. My mother taught that Argentine lesson so many times that I am sure she didn't remember her own exact words when Jimmy Miller heard it. But he remembered.

His letter to her was brief. All it said was:

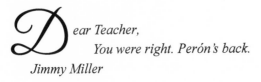

ear Teacher,
You were right. Perón's back.
Jimmy Miller

Senioritis

$\mathcal{L}$ ast Wednesday, I think, I can't remember, I went to yoga at our Carnegie Library. I hadn't been in a long while and knew my exercise might take a toll on me the next day. I am sixty-four. I am now considered a senior citizen. But my instructor once said in the past something about muscle memory. Do you know what that is? If you are like me, I don't want you to have to think too hard, let me help you recall.

Muscle memory has been used synonymously with motor learning. Motor leaning is a form of procedural memory that involves consolidating a specific motor task into memory through repetition. When a movement is duplicated over time, a long-term muscle memory is created for that task. Because of this repetition, the muscle allows it to be performed without conscious effort, decreases the need for attention, and creates maximum efficiency within the motor and memory systems. Examples of this are found in many everyday activities that become automatic and improve with practice, such as riding a bike, playing a musical instrument, typing on a keyboard, dancing, or typing in your PIN. I am glad my muscles remember the yoga moves because my brain seems to be slowing down.

Uh, where was I going with this? Oh yeah. I was talking about Wednesday.

Seniors are given discounts at certain stories on Wednesdays. Except at Kroger. They have stated that since they have low prices every day, there is no longer any need to give seniors an extra five percent off their purchases. Well, that's what I heard. But I don't know if I remember that correctly. But that same Wednesday after yoga, I went to the grocery to make a few purchases. These days, I mostly carry my list. But should I run in for a small number of items, I alphabetize them in my head.

Let's say I need bread, milk, lettuce, Cokes, cookies, and potatoes. I'd have to put them in alphabetical order to remember them: bread, Cokes, cookies, lettuce, milk, and potatoes. I'm going to get that wrong, so to help me, I shorten the list to the first letter of each word, as in b, c, c, l, m, p. And then I sometimes make a sort of anagram: bcclamp—bread, cookies, cokes, lettuce, *and* milk, potatoes. Well, I need more help, so I start singing it in my head. You know how you can remember the words to songs from decades before even if you haven't heard them in a long time? That's because words set to music help to build memory. I read that somewhere in my education courses but I can't tell you where. No, really. I can't tell you. I might sing—and I sing this out loud, mind you, but softly to myself—B-cclamp, cclamp, cclamp, cclamp. It has a nice beat. Like on American Bandstand, I'd give it a 6.

Oh, I failed to remember something else I needed to add to my list at the last minute and it's, "Don't forget at checkout to say, 'I am a senior,' so I can get that five percent discount." Now the B-cclamp has turned into B-cclamps. I'm alphabetizing, shortening, anagramming, singing and beat-boxing that bcclamps meter in my head while shopping. I choose my items, place in my buggy, get in checkout line, line my items up by cold purchases and regular purchases—to help the bagger—and as they are sliding on down the belt, I am pulling out my charge card from my Wonder-Bra-Purse, chatting with the friendly cashier, and yes, it's Wednesday, so you know where I am going with this, and then I fail to mention, "I am a senior!"

You'd think they'd notice.

I think I missed out on $1.23 after all that memorization, but I don't recall.

Since this essay, I have now heard that several grocery store chains have done away with any kind of senior discount on Wednesdays.

Senioritis, Part 2

I've had senioritis. I bet you have also. Like the shingles virus after it first surfaces, I think it can lie dormant in your system until it rears its ugly head decides later. What is it, you ask? Senioritis is a colloquial term here in the United States to describe the decreased motivation towards studying and is displayed by students who are nearing the end of high school, or college, even graduate school, or towards the end of a school year in general. The word *senior* is combined with the suffix *-itis*, which technically denotes inflammation but is assumed to mean a common illness.

My first bout with senioritis was in high school. Although never a studious pupil, it probably wasn't even noticed that I wasn't paying much attention those last few months before graduation. Heck, I wasn't paying much attention during any of those four years of high school at all. I was all about the pageantry of high school. I wasn't thinking that the purpose of high school was to ensure you into a great college. However, I did get in one. This was the 1970s. Lots of students who might have gone to a regular college went to Vietnam University. That meant there were lots of openings for poor students like me. I eventually got my act together after some more maturation and finding a major that interested me and that I wanted to pursue.

But this delayed senioritis is what bothers me now. It's creeping up on me again. This time, I am not lazy or uninterested. I care. But it doesn't. As my mother quoted from Bette

Davis, which I had to look up because I didn't remember, "Getting old ain't for sissies."

Well, you can't cry, so you have to laugh, and Jerry Seinfeld, my comic hero, has a routine on it. Let's begin:

"When did old people decide to back out of their driveway anymore not looking back? They think, 'I'm old and I'm coming back.' Old people in Florida drive slow and sit slow, so the state flag of Florida should be a steering wheel with two knuckles on it. And watch out for that left turn signal from seniors which they turned on as they left their house that morning. It's a legal term now in Florida known as the 'eventual left turn' and may be used that week or any following year in a senior's life."

My friend, Susan, who gave me permission to use her name and this story, used humor in a unique experience of her own. Her parents were shopping one day at one of the big-box stores. Both of retirement age, although I think her father said he'll never retire, were leaving the store and heading to their car in the large parking lot. Her father advanced on ahead of her mother to unlock their parked car. He'd help place groceries and other items in the hatch or backseat when she followed with the buggy.

Her mother made no misstep in the parking lot except to be in the wrong place at the wrong time. A young adult driver with baby in tow was pulling out of her space and knocked Susan's mother down on the pavement. Her glasses flew off as well as one shoe, she bruised her ribs, earned a cut above her eye, and hurt her hand trying to prevent her fall. Of course, the driver was shaken and tried to help, as well as other patrons of the store who were in the parking lot at the time. Refusing an ambulance, her husband drove her to the emergency room at the hospital for treatment. Hand in sling and much therapy to come, she should be alright.

Since this happened soon after the Christmas holidays, my friend couldn't help thinking of the song *Grandma Got Run Over by a Reindeer*, of which she penned this poem:

*G*randma got run over by a large car
     When she and Grandpa left the store.
     You can say there's no such thing as bad luck,
But I doubt they'll go to Walmart anymore.

*S*he was all done with her shopping
     And just wanted to go home
When that car backed up and whacked her.
We were glad she wasn't alone.

*P*eople ran to her and helped her
     As she lay there in a mound
With her broken hand and glasses,
They helped her get up off the ground.

*G*randma got run over by a large car
     When she and Grandpa left the store.
     You can say there's no such thing as bad luck,
But I doubt they'll go to Walmart anymore.

*T*he cut above her eye was bleeding,
     So, they drove to the ER
To stitch her up and splint her.
Hopefully, she will not have a scar.

*S*he's banged up good, poor Grandma,
And we think she'll be okay.
But we're grateful that dear Grandpa
Was there to help her out on that day.

*G*randma got run over by a large car
When she and Grandpa left the store.
You can say there's no such thing as bad luck,
But I doubt they'll go to Walmart anymore.

*T*oday she's going to the doctor
To see about her hand
And find out if she'll need surgery.
To make it better, is what's planned.

*E*ven though it scared them both.
But after all it's turned out all right.
And we don't have to worry
She's not ready to depart without a fight.

*I*t wasn't the elderly that had a case of senioritis.
Our baby-mama driver had a touch of it. It can
come in all forms of absent-mindedness and motivation. You
better watch out. It can sneak up behind you.

Characters

*H*ow did it come to this?

On November 7, 2017, Aatif Sulleyman with the *Independent* wrote, "Twitter is dropping its 140-character tweet limit for almost all users around the world, following just over a month of testing. The micro-blogging site, which has 330 million monthly active users, is increasing the limit to 280 characters for all languages where 'cramming' is an issue. It's a huge change for the site and Twitter said the move should also help users gain more followers and engage more with others."

I must say I just enjoyed reading in the *Newnan Times-Herald* the Year in Review section in December 31, 2017 paper. By month, the news was presented in capsule form— like Twitter. It published highlights of the most outstanding reporting in our community this past year. It was easy and quick to read. It presented the hot topics for the year in a concise way, like a student who would have to present his/her topic sentence of their next paper to their English teacher to see if the educator would allow it.

I blame this development on *Sesame Street*. Through my brain study as a former teacher for Gifted students, I learned that the adult brain can only grasp new information for twenty minutes at a time before the mind starts to wander. That's why your minister's sermon opening presentation catches your attention but twenty minutes in the sermon, your brain gravitates on to others things, like where to go to lunch or what you have to buy at the grocery store later.

Sesame Street, introduced November 10, 1969, knew about the attention span of toddlers and offered them tinier bits of information to absorb for their age. And some preschoolers of that era, Jack Dorsey (born 1976), Isaac "Biz" Stone (born 1974), and Evan Williams (born 1972), invented Twitter on March 21, 2006.

In the newspaper business, for hard news, we are supposed to write the most important information upfront, in the first paragraph, really, by presenting right off the bat who, what, when, where, why, and sometimes how. The reporter and publisher want an instantly readable and well-written story with those parameters. If it is, it will make the reader want more. But space is always the most precious commodity in newspapers and that's why the most important info has to be told first. You never know how long a reader will continue to read and where you editor is going to have to cut off your writing for space.

Plus, that twenty-minute rule. Will the mind wander and not care anymore if it is too long? Novels are different. They are supposed to elaborate all over the place. But journalism doesn't have that luxury.

I once taught a poetry lesson in British literature around the poem by Thomas Hardy entitled *The Darkling Thrush*. It represents his bleak reflections—with a bit of hope—on the eve of the twentieth century. A thrush is having a hard time adjusting to the winter. Although he writes the bird as joyful, the situation is bleak and he is vulnerable to the cold and harsh climate. The poem packed a lot into its thirty-two stanzas: irony, alliteration, rhyming, imagery, setting, etc. It may have been short but its theme was noteworthy.

Before our next test, I was emphasizing the literature that we had read and the reason this poem was notable. But for some reason, with all the other prose and poetry they read and had to learn, this one slipped through the cracks and they just couldn't remember what it was about. I mentioned all the literary terms above, told them about the struggles of the bird and its symbolism, and all the other meaningful thoughts the poet wanted us to know about looking back to the past century and looking ahead to a new one.

Nope, they didn't recall. Finally, I just blurted out, "You don't remember it? We spent an entire class period on that lesson about that bird." Then I said, "Okay. The bottom line of the poem was bird survives winter."

That simple. And then the commotion began, "Is that all?"

"We went through an entire English class on that?"

"That's it?"

"Why didn't you just say that was what it was about instead all that rig-a-ma-role?"

That's why Twitter is popular. Those brought up on *Sesame Street* are used to receiving information quicker. Both my Millennial sons were never without a computer in the home…instant informational gratification. I've worried about that a bit. My oldest told me his whole lifetime has been about technological advancements happening at rapid speed. They have come to expect it. So why shouldn't they send out their ideas the same way? It's all they've ever known…and in my opinion, it all started with *Sesame Street*.

The Augusta
Masters

*A*zaleas, pimento cheese sandwiches, and golf. It's the Masters in Augusta this week and a couple of things come to mind.

The Augusta National Golf Club, located in Augusta, Georgia and host to the Masters Tournament, is one of the most famous golf clubs in the world. Founded by Robert Tyre Jones, Jr. and Clifford Roberts, and designed on the former Fruitland Nursery site by Jones and Alister MacKenzie, the course opened for play in January 1933. Since 1934, the Augusta National Golf Club has played host to the Masters Tournament, one of the four major championships in professional golf. It is the only major played each year at the same course. In 2009, it was the number one ranked course in *Golf Digest*'s list of the one hundred greatest American courses.

It's been described as the toughest ticket in sports, and only Augusta National officials know how many Masters Tournament badges and practice round tickets are issued. And they aren't saying. Because of its popularity, even if more could be produced, it still wouldn't satisfy demand.

But that wasn't always the case. There were plenty to be had up until the 1960s. Then in 1966, the tournament sold out for the first time. A waiting list was created in 1972. Attending the Masters, despite the scarcity of tickets, is a bucket list item whether you are a golfer or not.

My dad loved golf and I loved golf because my dad loved golf. Hubby plays golf. My long-time college boyfriend played golf and his dad also played. Lucky enough to be members, this family paid the steep club dues for decades to Augusta National to be able to obtain four coveted badges for the yearly tournament. They enjoyed the four days of rounds following their favorite pro.

I've been twice.

And this enviable tournament was created by our Georgia boy, Bobby Jones. Jones (1902-1971) was an amateur golfer and one of the most influential figures in the history of the sport. With his input in founding and designing the course and co-founding the golf tournament, the innovations that he introduced at the Masters have been copied by virtually every pro-golf tournament in the world.

Jones, a lawyer by profession, was the most successful amateur golfer ever to compete at a national and international level. At his peak, 1923-1930, he dominated top-level amateur competitions and successfully competed against the world's best professional golfers. The era's top pros, Walter Hagan and Gene Sarazen, were often beaten by Bobby Jones.

Jones is most famous for his "Grand Slam" victories in all four major golf tournaments held in the United States and United Kingdom in a single calendar year (1930). In all, Jones played in thirty-one majors. He retired from competition at the age of twenty-eight but continued to earn significant money from golf after that as an instructor and equipment designer. He did come out of retirement in 1934 to play in the Masters and continued playing in Augusta on an exhibition basis until 1948. He played his last round of golf at East Lake Golf Club, his home course in Atlanta, on August 18, 1948.

Recently, while on book tour, I met an Atlanta gentleman, born and bred, and as he put it, "with a silver spoon in my mouth." His parents were members of East Lake Golf Club. In passing, he told me about his playing golf as a young man and now how his father was surprised he was not a better golfer than he was. He insisted that he really hadn't played much golf since taking lessons around the age of five at East Lake. He mentioned he would be a better player had he kept it up.

His father then added, "But still. You should be better at this game than you are because you took lessons from Bobby Jones."

What's Your
Excuse?

*A*fter college, I dated a guy who really was the epitome of a Southern gentleman. They say if you want to see what kind of gentleman your date really is—one not just showing off while dating, but one of real character—just look at how he treats his mama. I didn't have to go far to find that out in the 1970s because he was still living with his mother…and sister. As a matter of fact, many of our dates were with his mother and sister. What was I missing here?

That family was adorable. His father had died before I met him so I don't know that back story, but I did know he was looking after his mother and sister since he was gone. And he didn't place a step out of line the whole time around any of these women, including me. A real honorable man— courteous, man of his word, polished, and definitely a dandy dresser. I think he let me have my way a lot so I liked him.

His mother had a stack—*stack*—of unfinished school excuses on monogrammed note cards. They told me about them and I had to see them. They pulled out a kitchen drawer and then a ton of initialed card spilled out because there were so many. They were all blank except for the identical verbiage already printed out on the note, and they read: "Please excuse [name of my date], as he…"

That last part was left blank to be filled in as needed: "… as he had to go to the dentist," "…as he had a sore throat," "…as he was working as a page at the state Capitol for our state representative while the legislature was in session," or something else truthful and honest. It was never something like, "...as he couldn't get out of the bed when the alarm went off four times no matter how much I yelled at him to get his sorry ass out of bed because we know he doesn't like school and was just pretending to be sick," or "...as he knew he had that English paper due today deciphering quotes from *Hamlet*, which he knows was assigned three weeks ago and still did not prepare to have them ready today." And believe me, it would never have been one of those. The whole family was as honest as the day was long.

So having them printed out with a partial explanation was just a way to keep Mom from having to write more than was necessary. Back in the late sixties and early seventies, there weren't many trying to pull the wool over the school's eyes. Teachers and administrators were appreciated, and this family respected respect. They just didn't think that way.

Then again, it only takes one that makes one stop and think...maybe?

I learned about another student who, in 1969, was writing his own notes without his mother's knowledge, much less approval. One of my friends had this sneaky year-younger brother who was the last of four kids and whose parents were totally tired of having to keep up with all the children's school activities when her fourth and last one attended. In other words, she had no idea of his mischievous nature. He was pulling good grades, didn't get into trouble because he knew how to play everyone—learned how to manipulate from watching his older siblings in operation—and worked all these talents to his advantage. But he was still in the ninth grade and didn't have all his skills honed yet.

He wrote a note to the front office in his best mother's handwriting one day trying to excuse himself in his mother's "voice." And it read:

*D*ear Assistant Principal,
     I am writing this note to excuse my son, [his name here], for his absence last Friday. I kept him home all day because he was sick having symptoms of diarrea (sic). Your counselor must have been mistaken when he was out buying school supplies for his department and mentioned to you that he saw [his name here] hanging around the Skate-or-Bowl bowling alley next to the Dairy Queen on 4th Avenue around lunchtime. I suppose your counselor must have driven through the fast food restaurant to pick himself up some lunch while he was away from school running errands and when stopping to relay his meal order through the speaker thought he saw [his name here] just about to go in the bowling alley. This must be impossible because [his name here] was awfully sick all day until he got better in the afternoon and I let him go to track practice.

*H*is mother,
          Mrs. [His Name Here's Last Name]

"Boom!"
Says Auburn Coach
Gus Malzahn

*a*n NCAA football champion has been crowned. Football is over for 2017. Way to go SEC!

But while all the fussing, fighting, and finger-pointing was going on during the regular schedule, I was struck by one fan's unnecessary disappointment in general, and it was for his alma mater. I am a fan of that school. My undergraduate degree was from Georgia Southern University when there was no football program. I studied at the University of Georgia for my master's. Afterwards, I married an Auburn man. And I became a good Auburn wife, too. No house divided. I may have been a devout Georgia fan when we married, but I quickly became the perfect Auburn spouse. Why? Here's my rationalization:

- Playing and not really studying is a rite of passage in undergraduate school.
- In graduate school, you have to study to maintain that B average. You love your school but not much time to play and get too attached.
- When Auburn husband came into the picture, I acquiesced to keep harmony. And most importantly, he pays for all my charge card expenses, which makes me happy. Also, you never know which bunch of eighteen-to-twenty-year-old boys will show up on any given Saturday, so I shouldn't be too obsessed about football.

But I really do love football, probably because my dad coached all high school sports after his stint with the Chicago Cubs, which was interrupted by WWII.

And when I heard uncalled-for digs about a good coach, I became irked. I remember my mother sharing this story: After my dad quit coaching and teaching, he went into another profession but still called the football plays from the press box and refereed high school basketball games. One time, a booster was either oblivious or didn't care that the ref's wife was sitting behind him during a basketball game my dad was working. He objected to dad's calls and was letting everyone in the stands know it. But being the lady she was, she kept silent.

I am not that lady. Oh, I was brought up to be a Southern Belle, but like Scarlett O'Hara, I will speak my mind. More likely than not, I will prank somebody to get my point across. And I did with our friend.

It concerns Auburn's football coach. We SEC schools can't all win every game. Toppling the #1 and #2 teams in the nation *in one season* is huge, and this fan should be happy, but all season he wanted to ditch Malzahn. I wanted to teach him a lesson.

This friend is a fraternity brother of my husband's. He pays big bucks for the scholarship section seating at Jordan-Hare Stadium. You know about the scholarship section, don't you? Your food comes "free." You have a great view right under the press box. You don't have to walk around those spiral ramps a zillion times. Life is good up there. I've been a few times. Once you've been there, you really don't want to go back to general seating. It sounds a lot like the advice I received as a virgin from a non-virgin friend, "Once you've had it, you want it." She suggested I not do "it."

So, he is special. Really...and that's fine. I guess that

gives him the right to spout off because he is paying a lot of money for not only all that comfort at the football games but also to the university scholarship committee, which, truth be told, some probably goes to the athletic department. But I heard about his remarks and decided to see if he could take my frivolity about his comments.

This Auburn Tigers fan received an Auburn designed Christmas card from Head Coach Gus Malzahn. The holiday greeting not only was personally signed by Malzahn, but also had a handwritten note in the card from the coach. It thanked him for his endowment to the scholarship fund and his continued support of "all things Auburn" and was looking forward to next season. Auburn Athletics' street address was posted in the return address corner and the post mark was from Opelika, Alabama, which was as close to Auburn as I could get it at the time to mail it.

And at the bottom, with the coach's scrawny and almost undecipherable signature, was the word which he is famous for saying and which he demonstrates when something exciting happens for Auburn on the sideline of all the television games:

"*Boom!*"

Paper Trail

*I*n the 1950s and 1960s, paper dolls were where our little girl imaginations played...whether it be Betsy McCall or the Lennon Sisters. Starting in 1951, and lasting until around 1995, Betsy McCall paper dolls were printed in most issues of *McCall's* magazine, and in the '50s and '60s, I cut out the printed doll and her clothing from the monthly magazine. I didn't pay the extra ten cents in 1957 and twenty-five cents in 1967 for Betsy to be mounted to cardboard. I carved out a cardboard likeness of her pose for that month and glued it to the thin previously paper cut-out Betsy. I could attach her clothes by adding tabs to her clothes and cut them out to use to fold down her outfits to the paper doll. Betsy usually came dressed in a camisole and you just added the various outfits over her paper frame. She might have a summer shorts with a coordinating top outfit, and also shoes to match. Or a dress that wasn't too fancy but fancier than what one would wear to school. I think there were two, maybe three, different changes of clothes for your doll each month. And when Betsy arrived in *McCall's* magazine, she was displayed in different poses. She became so popular that various sized vinyl dolls of her likeness were produced by American Character Dolls and Ideal.

The Lennon Sisters were another famous paper doll undertaking. One learned about the Lennon sisters through *The Lawrence Welk Show*. For thirteen years, from 1955 to 1968, Diane, Peggy, Kathy, and Janet appeared regularly on his Saturday night program. In 1959, the group's set came in a tri-fold book with four dolls and twenty pages of clothes. The two nine-by-twelve tri-fold inner pockets allowed one to store their clothes. There was also an outer pocket for the dolls. Printed on heavy cardboard, they were ready to punch out and play without making your own cardboard back. The dolls ranged in size—just like the sisters—from seven and a half inches to nine inches. They even came with stands! That was a plus when playing with all four. The set included eighty-four pieces of clothing and accessories for the girls.

Although not a paper doll, the princess of dolls during that time was Barbie. I had several of different hair color. And a couple of Ken dolls. I had Barbie's sister, Skipper, too. When it came to accessories, I owned lots of her casual dresses, shoes, hats, slacks, swimsuits, her pink car, the Barbie board game, and even her cardboard paper house with furniture for every room. There were no homemade or snatched-from-another-doll-toy knockoffs. Everything was original Barbie, made by Mattel paraphernalia.

I planned a wedding with Barbie and Ken and invited all my Barbie doll owners to dress up and attend. I bought the Wedding Day Barbie bride's dress, which came out in 1961. It was a silk-like full white dress with a large poof skirt. She had a flower designed taffeta overlay over the skirt and on her long sleeves. Barbie had a pearl halo-like veil made of taffeta looming large behind her hair, which did not cover her face, and she wore a pearl necklace, pearl stud earrings, white high-heel shoes, and carried a pink bouquet.

One friend's mother made two wedding cakes for the attendees: a miniature one for the dolls and another for my living and breathing girlfriends. Although Skipper was her maid-of-honor, I do not remember what she wore, but Ken looked like Rock Hudson or Don Draper from *Mad Men* in his black tux. Everyone in the audience looked alike except for the variety of different Mattel-designer dresses.

At the reception, the bride and groom pretended to cut the little cake and drink pink punch. The live audience did enjoy real sweets and libation. I took pictures with my 960 Kodak Brownie Cresta 3 camera which used 120 film and produced six-by-six images. The Fotomat wasn't available in 1963 to just drive-thru and drop off my film, so I think we took our film to the drugstore and had them develop it somehow. But I did create a wedding album for Barbie and Ken.

They did not tell me where they were going on their honeymoon, probably in my closet, but they did drive off in Barbie's pink convertible and they lived in her pink cardboard house when they were let out to play. But poor Ken, living in a pink world, since it was Barbie's favorite color.

"She Wore an

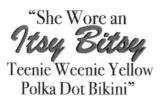

Teenie Weenie Yellow
Polka Dot Bikini"

*H*ubby and I moved after my father passed so we could keep an eye on my mother, who was "getting on up there" in years and living all alone on our thirty-acre homestead. It wasn't a farm as we didn't keep cattle, but we did have a pond with fish in it. Because we were in such close proximity to Atlanta, the housing boom spread in the late 1980s, and developers found out about how attractive our county was and how convenient to Atlanta it was. Soon, lots of Boomers were living in "bedroom communities" like ours because of the quality of life for their families outside of the city.

A major Atlanta developer was looking to build a three-hundred-fifty-home neighborhood, but he had to have a zoning variance for it to be worth his money and time. My county was still pretty archaic in our ordinances because it hadn't been discovered yet. But now here it was. The Planning and Zoning Recommendation Board denied this builder's request to change things for the future. A meeting with the County Board of Commissioners who would have the last say was being held one afternoon and I pondered whether I should attend to speak on his behalf regarding his request to build. I had a vested interest in this project. Building this new subdivision would make his development my back-door neighbor.

I knew about this builder. And I knew about his possible seller. I had seen the quality that went into his product and could count on it. The sellers? Not so much. If not him, who?

That's what worried me. So I made the effort to show up for the board meeting. There were the usual suspects lined up to be nay-sayers about the project. There was Mrs. Small-Town-Real-Estate-Developer, there were stuffy old men who did not want to see change regarding their pasture properties—if they only knew how much they could laugh their way to the bank —as well as others. I, on the other hand, had left my small town, gone to the big city, and was back home again. I wanted progress. I, too, was selling real estate and knew that having this well-known developer almost in my backyard was a good thing. So, I attended the meeting.

Like everyone else, I stood up and voiced my opinion. They were negative about his coming to join our little group of great folks, but I suggested since I had thirty acres which would abut the proposed development, my opinion should carry more weight. I guess it did. The three-member board voted two to one in his favor.

The next day, I received a phone call to ask if I would be interested in interviewing for the real estate agent's job in that designer community. I loved the broker I was working with and asked her if I should go and she really encouraged me to try. There was no competition. They offered the job to me as soon as I walked in the door. Oh, it might have looked like a setup, but believe me, my thoughts and actions to push the variance through were pure as the driven snow. How did I know how the board would vote?

But because it did happen, and I suppose to thank me for my participation, I accepted. And it was a great job. The community grew steadily and was designed for families with children as it had an Olympic pool for swimming meets, slides, baby pools, and a clubhouse for all. Those were pretty snazzy neighborhoods he was building all around Atlanta, and this time it was our turn.

One particular story surfaced around the pool house. A gorgeous woman, originally from France, parked herself at the pool almost every day. This gal was young, beautiful, and had a figure that was a twelve on a scale of one to ten. And while sunning, her bathing suit consisted of a thong.

This made the adolescent boys happy, but you know who was not happy? Their parents. Mothers became concerned. There were whispers by the pool about how to solve this problem. There were no covenants for this kind of thing. All summer they had to endure her bare-assed nakedness being flaunted in front of them. So, one mom, who had a rather large body type and a larger-than-life personality to go with it, finally found the nerve to speak to this goddess. In her large and flowing muumuu, she approached the temptress while she nonchalantly sun-bathed. The other mothers coiled behind the waterslide.

"Excuse me. I have to mention that the way you appear here at the pool is offensive to me," said the overloaded woman.

Not missing a beat, this non-inhibited European-minded woman had the best comeback. She responded, "Well, the way you appear here at the pool is offensive to *me!*"

When I'm *Sixty-Four*

*E*ven Paul McCartney at the young age of seventeen was thinking ahead when writing *When I'm 64*.

I am sixty-four. If I am lucky, I'll make it to sixty-five in a few months if I don't have a heart attack first. I've been raising hell with all my screaming behavior, growling, and gritting my teeth whenever I am bombarded by all the phone calls, letters, discussions, and decisions regarding Medicare. Can't they leave me alone?

I'm taking Welch poet Dylan Thomas's approach, "Do not go gentle into that good night."

I should make them aware of how WHO, the World Health Organization, describes sixty-five. They declare that sixty-five is still considered young. This wasn't always the case. Before, based on the Friendly Societies Act (1875) in Britain, "old" was defined by the age of fifty. The UN has not adopted a standard criterion, but lately, sixty years of age was referred to as the border age of the word "old." WHO, however, recently conducted new research, and according to average health quality and life expectancy, it now defines new criterion that divides human age as follows:

0-17 years old: underage

18-65 years old: youth or young people

66-79 years old: middle-aged

80-99 years old: elderly or senior

100+ years old: long-lived elderly.

I think I like being thought of as youthful, although I sometimes certainly don't feel that way.

But here in the United States, as of January 2011, and as part of the Affordable Care Act, the Medicare Annual Wellness visit was initiated. This yearly Medicare benefit includes the creation of a personalized prevention plan and detection of possible cognitive impairment. The Alzheimer's Association assembled a group of practicing expert clinicians to make consensus proposals for an effective, practical, and easy process for detecting cognitive impairment decline in the primary care setting. An algorithm was approved which incorporates patient history, clinician observations, and concerns expressed by the patient, family, or caregiver. Because of the use of a cognitive assessment instrument, improvements can be made in the detection of the dementia in one's primary care setting. The test can be administered in five minutes or less by a physician or other trained staff.

Oh, goodie. It will be my turn soon.

In the meantime, I have been forewarned. A teacher friend who is three years older told me about her first-time assessment. She was asked to draw a very large circle on an even larger piece of paper. It was to include a dot in the center of the circle. This circle and dot were to eventually represent a clock. She was then to add numbers on the face of the clock. Afterwards, she was to draw the hour and minute hands to represent ten minutes until eleven o'clock. On her first test after her sixty-fifth birthday, she drew a large circle and dot, and while starting to place the numbers in their designated spots, she began at the top of her clock with the number one. Immediately realizing her mistake and knowing she should have drawn twelve instead at the top of the clock face, she needed to start over, but did not have another sheet. She turned her paper over and drew everything in correctly.

In another year and another doctor, she was asked to accomplish the same cognitive test. Like the previous examination, her paper was large and her clock face took up most of the paper. Again, the instructions included for her to draw the clock hands to represent ten minutes until eleven o'clock. Having experience in this directive, she beautifully designed her clock and all the elements requested. She first placed the number twelve at the top and then surrounded the circle with three, six, and nine. Afterwards, she placed the remaining numbers evenly in between. When her MD returned to check her work, she saw the delight on her doctor's face. The physician mentioned not only was it gorgeous—my friend is an artist—but it was also perfectly proportioned. This doctor continued to rave about her work.

Dumbfounded, my friend questioned, "How hard can this be? Surely everyone knows how to do that."

The doctor responded by shaking her head. "No, not really. Seventy-five to eighty percent do not get it right."

"Get out!" her patient exclaimed. "You've gotta be kidding. What do they do wrong?"

"Even people who seem really 'with it' mess up," her medical doctor responded. "One person recently drew in the numbers correctly and then put the hour hand and minute hand *outside* of the clock. Another patient drew more than two hands, and all the hands were the same length so it was impossible to determine the hour or minute. There was one person who drew the hands on the clock to read eleven minutes until ten, not the correct instruction of ten minutes until eleven. Still another designed a rectangle, as in a digital clock, and drew in 10:11."

Now I know what I have to look forward to.

Happy birthday to me.

The Tooth
Fairy

*T*here is a pattern, a common denominator, and similarity to a few successful and important people that I have paid attention to for some time. All are in government in some form, so you'd think I'd mention strength of character, high morals, good judgment and such. Nope. None of those. It's their big teeth.

Case study one: the James Earl Carter family.

People would say that Amy was the one with the large set of teeth for such a little girl. The reason for that is simple: she was a little girl and hadn't grown into her teeth yet. Of course they appear larger for the young. Teeth are made for a full-size person. Now her mouthful fits into that same big smile. But I say it's not Amy, it is Jeff, one of three Carter boys. He is the one carrying their genetic make-up for a larger set of teeth and jaw.

Case study two: the Bill Clinton family.

Here is another important family in politics whose daughter is the one loaded with the ivories, not the parents. Chelsea didn't seem to really grow out of them from childhood either, do you think? Since heredity has everything to do with what you might receive, you'd think you'd see something in the Clinton family. Maybe that physical characteristic is further back than just her immediate kin.

Case study three: the Joseph Kennedy family.

In this case, almost every Kennedy has a bundle. Many people inherit large teeth from one side of the family and small jaws from the other side of the family. This causes severe crowding. Personally, I think the Kennedys collected this DNA from both Joe and Rose. They both had lots of teeth…lots of long, white, wide teeth. It's the first thing I notice when looking at most all of them.

Case study four: the British Windsor family.

Now William is cute as a tick, but come on, he's got some long incisors. I don't think you'll see that on the Spencer side of the family. Look at his Aunt Anne, Queen Elizabeth I's only daughter. Now there is a chipmunk mouth. I take *Majesty* magazine and believe me, there are some past relatives with the same portion. And you know in the nineteenth century they were still marrying their cousins, so I guess that answers that about dominant gene coming from both sides of a family. They didn't have great dental care for the longest time. If they had a good dentist over there, one might have been able to help with braces or resetting their jaw. Anne's two offspring also have pretty big kissers, and Margaret, Elizabeth's sister, had children with some choppers as well.

Case study five: the J. Donald Trump family.

Is it just me? Am I wrong in this comparison? What do these political dynasties have in their water? Donald, Jr., Eric, and Ivanka. I swear, the first thing I notice are their mouths. Is this an illusion? Is it because their heads are small so their teeth look big? I read fathers passing their teeth to daughters can make the females teeth look like Chicklet gum. And if mothers pass their teeth to sons, they might look like corn kernels when the boys are adults. I don't see this trait in The Donald or Ivana.

Having big teeth is called macrodontia. It's genetic and found in many African Americans. The ideal mouth is not too far forward, both the upper and lower teeth show, and there is not much gum showing; this is where the tooth size works out okay.

So, what does a Tooth Fairy pay for these large teeth? Are they worth more? If so, in these cases, it's a good thing that these families are well off. They can help her out with the expense.

Dam It!

My family took two vacations to the Grand Canyon; once with only our oldest and another time with both boys. Both times we swung by Las Vegas, Nevada. My husband's mother lived in Las Vegas for a time. It was her kind of town: exciting, lots of people her age, and cheap meals for a retiree. She looked younger than her years and acted like it, too. When she was in her mid-seventies, she took a job in a gift shop at Caesar's Palace. It really was a good fit because she liked talking to people and all kinds of people came to the store to buy souvenirs. But let me make it clear, this job wasn't just some quaint little ole lady daytime job. Granny worked the night shift.

On the first trip, we flew into the Grand Canyon from Vegas in a de Havilland plane that seated eight. Going by plane shorted the five-hour trip by three hours, plus, getting closer to our destination, we flew at the rim's edge to get a bird's-eye view into the many canyons. Wearing earphones, the synchronized pre-recorded dialogue coincided with where we were in flight and the narrator told us to look left or right to see this or that. That really was a neat experience, being guided like this on our trip. When we reached the canyon, we stayed at a hotel on the South Rim overnight.

Our second trip included a tour of Hoover Dam. The Hoover Dam is described by the US Department of the Interior's Bureau of Reclamation as "a testimony to a country's ability to construct monolithic projects in the midst of adverse conditions. Built during the Depression, thousands of men and their families came to Black Canyon to tame the Colorado River. It took less than five years, in a harsh and barren land, to build the largest damn of its time. Now years later, Hoover Dam still stands as a world-renowned structure. The Dam is a National Historic Landmark and has been rated by the American Society of Civil Engineers as one of America's Seven Modern Civil Engineering Wonders."

One elderly man operating the elevator to send people up and down the structure had a good time with his title: Dam Operator. He was very friendly and folksy and gave historic information about the dam's operations. I thought, *Wow, what a terrible job to have to do this all day: deliver people up and down in the elevator and tell the same stupid jokes. The history part was interesting but how many times could you pretend to enjoy doing it? I remember having to teach the same lesson plan three times a day and I got pretty bored by the third round. And he's been doing this for years, possibly. Poor guy. Well, at least he has a job.*

I leaned into my eldest, who was about ten the first time we toured this site, and even though the elevator was somewhat crowded, I whispered in his ear so no one else would hear, "See, honey? This is what you do when you don't have a good education." I am a teacher. I couldn't help myself to make a point when I could about more offerings and choices one might have with a better education. I didn't want him to have to resort to doing something so mundane for minimum wage and I wanted to make my point at this opportune time so he would remember it.

After getting off at ground level to take the tour, we thanked the gentleman and asked him how long he had worked there. I don't remember anything he said except he was a volunteer, had a Ph.D., and was a retired history professor from the University of Nevada at Las Vegas.

Well, shut my damn mouth.

Letter to the Editor
Sometime During
1991-1992

*D*ear Editor,

Please let me get this off my chest in this forum. Maybe others will understand if I do, and maybe even others will empathize with my situation, but even if they do not, I know I am going to feel better. I had not been myself. My fun-loving personality was gone. I was sad and so I turned to drugs for what I thought would help. They were prescription drugs. My doctor wanted me to take them, and because he and I both wanted success in my being happy, he prescribed a big dose for a long while.

I took them for a year. They obviously didn't help because I didn't receive the results I was hoping for. As a matter of fact, they made me worse. Much worse. They did not assist me in my struggle and I became more frustrated and angry. I became *really* angry. I was upset over every little thing—anything my husband did, whether he blew his nose, which, in my opinion, might have been too loud, or hearing his him chew every bite of food during dinner, or just even looking at me...I found fault in everything he said and did.

And it wasn't only my husband. My friends weren't behaving any better either. Their quirks bothered me. I didn't like being around them. I hid from my friends and quit enjoying life. I was depressed and I couldn't get out of it. My drug dependency increased. I was obsessed. Maybe taking more would do the trick. But it didn't. I absolutely wanted to randomly kill someone...just take a shotgun and blast away. It didn't matter who it was. I had all this pent-up rage inside me, I was miserable, and also unbearable to live with. I didn't understand what was happening to me or how I got this way.

And it's not the kind of drugs you might think. I was trying to get pregnant the second time around. My first pregnancy was a piece of cake. The second was not, and we upped my chances with the drug Clomid.

It is medication that is commonly used for treatment of infertility. Trying to have another baby was difficult and evading us for no reason. When Hubby and I wanted our first born, we just wished upon a star and bibbidy-bobbidy-boo, our first was conceived the first month of trying. Wanting to space my children three years apart, and because I was still young enough to think I had control of everything, we just couldn't make it happen. And we tried…for five years.

Clomid is also frequently used to stimulate extra follicles to develop in the ovaries of women who already ovulate without medications. I had one child. Why was this second so hard to come by? But what I didn't know until much later was that Clomid, although not a steroid, is still a performance enhancer and is a favorite of anabolic steroid users, like wrestlers, body builders, or other athletes, and we read about some of their bizarre and extreme behaviors.

No one told me about the "Clomid Crazies" side effects. One might experience anxiety, panic attacks, sleeping diffi-culties, insomnia, irritability, and mood swings. And I can attest to these symptoms being real. Friends knowing what I was going through trying to have our second child would be so sweet to say, "Oh, Lee. I wanted to tell you personally that my husband and I are pregnant with our fourth child. I wish it was you."

My irritated, angry, crazy, uncalled-for response? "I wish it was me, too."

Another said, "Please don't be sad. You have one beautiful, healthy child to be proud of."

"Oh, yeah? Well, you have three children. Which two would you get rid of?" Ouch.

I was as mean as a junkyard dog. I wanted to bite the head off the next person who just looked at me, much less spoke to me. Better yet, I wanted to just take a shotgun and kill them. Seriously. Not in a great mental state of mind, was I? I had commented that if I was on a jury where a wife of a certain age was going through the post-menopausal phase where her hormone levels were helter-skelter like mine was accused of killing her husband, I would have voted not guilty.

It was awful. I was awful.

So, Editor, because I behaved badly for a couple of years, I need to make amends. I did not know what I was doing to myself by taking those prescription drugs except trying to get a second baby to our home. I am asking forgiveness of all my friends, here and now, who put up with a shrew during that time. I was as wild as a banshee who wanted to tear into anyone who was trying to say or do the right thing for me but I wouldn't let them.

I hope they read this sincere apology here in the Letter to the Editor section. Thank you for the opportunity to try to make amends to any and all.

With remorse,

Lee St. John

P.S. We never had that child after all that trouble and yearning. But we were eventually blessed. We adopted the right one for us.

Whatever Works

I hated it when my mother used guilt to get me to behave. It was all about shame.

Whatever works.

I once had to fill out an application answering questions about what my family's discipline procedure was for my two-year-old. I was pretty nervous answering that inquiry because we were applying for next year's preciously few openings in our church's preschool program. There were only so many vacancies. But I also needed to be honest. I answered:

Whatever works.

He still got in.

I am not a real stickler for routine discipline. My line of thinking is "just behave." And personally, I don't like harsh training. I would rather be creative and slough off the hard approach to somebody or something else that might work. For instance, after taking our oldest, when he was around two, to the mall where he could run off if not watched because he wasn't holding my hand at all times, I had to eventually purchase a child restraint leash. Well, it wasn't called a leash, but that was what it was used for. It was a four-inch-wide fastener made with Velcro. Besides its extra secure closure, it also had extra-long shoulder straps when he wore heavy winter clothing. The swivel clip prevented strap tangles. It worked just like the one I use today when I walk my dog.

How embarrassing, really, but at least it was lightweight and washable—but come to think of it, so is my dog's. I bought into the company's advertisement about it allowing a child the freedom to explore while still remaining close. It slipped on easily and fastened in the back for effortless adjusting. Let's face it, it was a dog leash and I received lots of stares. But this child wanted to roam and I didn't have the heart to punish him. I remember how I felt when I was being chastised for something I didn't know I was doing wrong. Once wearing Red Goose's white classic high top baby walking shoes to church when I was around two, and before there were nurseries for young children to attend while their parents sat in the sanctuary for the sermon, I was trying to get comfortable and put my head in my mother's lap. With my restless nature, those hard-heeled shoes clunked all over that wooden pew and Mother had to get on to me so many times to be still and quiet. Not knowing I was disturbing the other parishioners but still being reprimanded, she later told me I said, "I don't want to come to church anymore." I think she bought some soft-soled Sunday shoes for me to wear after that.

Whatever works.

I didn't want my child leaving with a bad experience when he didn't know better and couldn't move about freely. And I don't think he knew he looked funny with that harness or that the other old-timer-parents doing their morning walks around the enclosed mall objected to my choice.

So, as he grew from two into three, and before attending public school, I was able to devise an idea that I put into motion. Since he wasn't recognizing but a few words here and there, I let the department store take the fall. I could take the leash off and just point to the discount tables that read *20% Off on Items at This Table Only*, or *Buy One, Get One Half-Off*, or *Markdowns – 70% Taken at Register*. I would walk him over, point to these signs, and say, "Look, honey!

The store is telling you to hold your mother's hand! They are in charge of telling us what to do, so we have to cooperate." He bought it.

Whatever works.

When I needed to get a point across or make sure my children heard the important piece of information I was saying, I asked them to repeat it back to me. If they could, then I knew they heard me and they processed the information.

Whatever works.

My dear friend used another tactic on her three children. You know how as mothers we just repeat and voice manners and good habits to our children all the time like, "Wash your hands before dinner," "Brush your teeth before you go to bed," or "Turn the light out and go to sleep!" With this woman having said stuff like that with her first child, her second and third children had already heard her commands so much that when it became their turn, they knew what she was going to say before she said it. So, whenever the situation arose with them, all she eventually had to say was this: "You just tell *me* what it is that I am about to say to you." It was stuck in their brains from it constantly being spoken before.

Whatever works.

"I Don't Know *Nothin'* 'bout *Birthin' Babies,*" said Prissy

*M*e either, Prissy. Or what I was supposed to do afterwards, either.

I had a C-section with our first born. I didn't know that was going to happen. Our birthing coach told us that one in ten couples would have one. There were ten couples in our birthing class. As the time approached for our turn to give birth, one couple had just had their first child with a C-section. I thought to myself, *There it is. There's the* one.

Best laid plans…

Even though we went through birthing class to learn about a natural delivery, I always knew I was going to have drugs. When my turn came, I got some. But the baby wasn't really ready for launch, and after seventeen hours, with part of that time connected to an epidural needle and drip, I was going to have to go for the C-section. Thinking he was just going to be a seven pound-something newborn, as time went on, his head was too big to come down the birth canal, his weight was finally to be determined to be over nine pounds, and we were now getting ready to have surgery; I had to have more drugs. Needless to say, I was out of it at time of delivery. I don't remember much. But earlier I was coherent enough in the process to remember to ask the anesthesiologist, who I met for the first time under these conditions, from which medical school had he graduated. That's always the question of any doctor I begin an association with. "Where did you go to medical school?" If I didn't like his answer, I could leave and find another doctor. However, what could I do about it now? Anyway, his answer was a good one.

Until all those drugs left my system, I was really in a funk. Although still in a stupor, I did remember about the two-week check-up for our newborn, although it took me a long to time to function at full capacity. When it became closer to the appointment, the pediatrician's office called to remind me and said, "You are scheduled to bring your baby in for his two-week exam tomorrow." I thought, *He's two weeks old already?*

On consultation day, mother said she would drive us there while Hubby was at work. Good. I had just recently had my stitches removed. In 1985, they stitched a C-section up with staples. I dressed our first born in something cute to be taken out in public, although I don't remember what it was. I placed him appropriately in the car seat and let Mother take the wheel. I might have taken a quick nap. When we arrived, I took him inside to the doctor's office at the appointed time and while there, something happened I hadn't thought of. They asked, "Where is your diaper bag?" What? I was supposed to bring a diaper bag? No one told me that. My telephone reminder said to bring in the baby for his two-week check-up. They didn't say, "…and your diaper bag, too." I just brought the baby. Since I was mostly sleep deprived, hurting from staple removal, and totally confused with this infant I knew nothing about, I honed in on the keys elements in that telephone conversation: appointment, exam, and bring baby. That's what they told me to transport.

They thought that was so funny. I was an idiot. But for the baby's sake we could solve any problem should it arise at the medical office—they had diapers of the right size for their patients and I was carrying the milk, so all was well. My mother hadn't even noticed I went without a diaper bag. It had been thirty-two years since she had a baby, and after all those years and no repeat children, she had forgotten, too. And to her credit, her job was to get us there safely. That's all she was thinking about. And she did a good job, too.

Me? Not so much.

Love It
or Leave It

*W*e are moving.

I'd say we are moving into a new home, however, that's not exactly correct. It is new to us but dates back to 1929. The last time we moved, it was to move to my current house, and that was fifteen years ago. Moving was difficult then. It's more difficult now because I am fifteen years older. And as my book title, *She's A Keeper!*, suggests, I've got to do something with all this accumulated stuff.

Should it stay or should it go? Help me out here, will ya?

1. I have a box filled with 45s. Groups such as The Beatles, The Dave Clark Five, Dino, Desi, and that third guy in their group, the Supremes, Temptations, Four Tops, and more. Sure, there was only one good song because we always ignored the B side, but shouldn't I keep them because they're original?

2. Old ice trays made of aluminum with the pull lever to crack the cubes open. They belonged to my mother. Will my kids ever see a tray like that again? I want them to see living history, you know.

3. Why I still have my parents' 1960s console TV set, I don't know. It was the kind where you only survived on four channels and there was no such thing as a remote back then. It's pecan-colored and

has a record player on one side. Do I dare throw
that away?

4. My first cootie-catcher. How do I know it's my
first? It has my first boyfriend's name from sixth
grade in one of the triangles, that's how.
That stays.

5. Who would want my set of World Book
encyclopedias? I guess they are a keeper. Ugh.

6. VHS player. No Beta for us. And all those
recorded tapes. Last night, Hubby and I watched a
few to decide which to keep because some of them
contained our children at their birthday parties,
playing ball, piano recitals, band recitals, jumping
on all the contraptions at our local gym, etc. Of
course, I wouldn't dare depart without those…nor
all my *The Bachelorette* shows from way back…
especially our Georgia Peaches seasons—DeAnna
Pappas, hometown honey, and Andy Dorfman,
Duluth, Georgia.

7. I found an old checkbook belonging to my dad.
You know my Millennial boys do not know about
such a thing. Should I keep it to show them
sometime?

8. Can someone develop that old film strip from the
1960s that I found in the very back of a cluttered
drawer? If they only still had those Kodak drive-
thru huts in the shopping strips' parking lot like
we used to, I might be able to get it developed.
Oh, wait a minute…I also found a Polaroid
picture, too. It's me with that sixth grade cootie-
catcher boyfriend. You know we weren't supposed
to really shake those Polaroids but we did anyway.
Keeping that for sure.

9. Uh-oh. I can't return this if I wanted to. It's a Blockbuster VHS: the original *Ghostbusters.* This is going over to the other house. I wonder if I paid the late fee. Oh, I see I didn't rewind it…there would have been another fee for that.

10. I never got around to getting this rotary dial phone down to our lake home while I was decorating it in mid-century modern. So, of course, it will be sent there as part of my *Mad-Men*-Don-Draper-esque décor. And it's English pea green. Yay, me! Remember answering the phone every time it rang because you never knew who could be calling? And that cord tangled a lot probably because you would twist it with your finger as you nervously talked to a cute crush…hint, hint—that cootie-catcher sixth grader.

Okay, so it's settled. Thanks for helping me decide "Should It Stay or Should It Go."

Help me again sometime?

The Shadow Knows
Leftover Laughter
from the Classroom

*P*ersuasion essay: Because we read this book for class, persuade someone in this timed essay to read *Dr. Jekyll and Mr. Hyde* by Robert Louis Stephenson by giving examples from the book of why they should.

I am a great *The Shadow* comic book fan; good and evil is something I know about. I mean, I like reading comic books. You can learn a lot from comic books or even cartoons. How many times did you hear classical music on Bugs Bunny? Lots. This is why I can relate to our book we read for class, *Dr. Jekyll and Mr. Hyde*.

This time, our teacher didn't show us a movie about it. I like it when she shows us the movie version. I get more out of it when I see the movie version. It fills in the gaps about the parts that I didn't read—I mean, didn't understand while reading the (Cliffs notes version) book. This was a good book.

Since good vs. evil is the main theme of the book and since I also like good vs. evil comic books, like Batman vs. anybody, Superman vs. anybody, The Green Lantern vs. anybody, Wonder Woman vs. anybody, and even all the new movies that are remakes from comic books, I liked this story very much and told all my friends about how we (had to) read it in English class, and although I didn't want to, I am glad I did because it was about good vs. evil.

For this timed test, I am supposed to write about good vs.

evil in *Dr. Jekyll and Mr. Hyde*. You might guess from the title that one was good and one was evil. But which one? Just like me, you will have to read the book (if you don't read the Cliffs notes) to find out much more, but I can share some things now.

Let me begin. Dr. Jekyll is a doctor and believes good and evil exists in everyone. That means you and me. I believe that to be true. We have our good side we show everybody and our bad side that we don't. Ok. I guess I will have to tell you a bit about the story, although I really wanted to keep you guessing. Dr. Jekyll conducts experiments and something happens to him when he does. This is one reason you should read this book…to find out why. And then when you do, you can tell me and we will both know. No, really, please tell me.

We didn't see the movie because there wasn't a more modern version to "capture our interests," our teacher said. I wouldn't have minded watching a 1941 version so long as I learned something more about this story. I like movies that are made from books and I think I would have learned something new.

Dr. Jekyll walks with a cane and that has something to do with the plot. But you will have to find that out for yourself. And there are drugs involved, so maybe this book shouldn't be on the approved reading list in the first place. I mean, how did this book get approved anyway? Should we be reading about people taking drugs in the nineteenth century? I don't care if the drug was prescribed, that is a big deal these days for vulnerable teens, like me, to learn about in books. I might tell my parents about how I shouldn't have been made to read this book because it had drugs in it and I am not supposed to know about drugs.

Our teacher called it a novella. Is that the feminine version for the masculine name, novel?

But my time is almost up as my teacher called out "ten minutes remaining" and grades are important to my parents, so I better keep writing because I don't think that idea of not reading this book well (at all) is going to work. This way, just by turning in an essay, I might get a 50 instead of a zero on this assignment. Anything is better than a zero. Trust me. Anyway, something happens that is shocking, then something else happens that is more shocking, lots of letters are exchanged because this story is way before email, and then at the end, the police get involved. I guess it is Scotland Yard because this book takes place in London, which I forgot to tell you earlier.

This is the kind of story that should be on ID Discovery TV. Then I'd be able to watch a screen version, which would help me a lot to understand all these twists and turns. Even with the (Cliffs) notes we took in class, I got lost. I have wrestling practice every day and when I get home I don't have time to read much. Every time I started reading I fell asleep. I really tried!

Our teacher says one more minute and our timed essay writing is up. So let me leave you with this:

"Who knows what evil lurks in the hearts of men? The Shadow knows." My favorite comic book, which I read every day.

ime!

The
"*Me, Too*"
Movement

$\mathcal{M}$e, too.

By now you've probably been made aware through all forms of social media of a groundswell that has erupted into our consciousness. It is called the Me, Too Movement. This movement of empathy is to empower women—although men are affected also—to reveal the extent of problems regarding sexual harassment and assault by showing how many people have experienced these events themselves. Anyone on social media who wishes to disclose that they, too, felt violated could write on Twitter, Instagram, Facebook, and other social platforms #MeToo to express solidarity about the widespread prevalence of these behaviors in the workplace. The idea of stating #MeToo started in 2006 but came to prominence after the public revelations of the 2017 sexual misconduct allegations against Harvey Weinstein, a former American film producer who co-founded Miramax, a Hollywood entertainment company.

There are dark places in our society. Recently, after attending the Erma Bombeck Writers Workshop for those who pen humor or human interest stories, I met Lauretta Hannon. She was on our workshop faculty for the weekend. Everyone—faculty, guest speakers, those attending—was there to help participants hone their skills in whatever creative medium we are currently undertaking—screen plays, blogs, newspapers, magazines, stand-up comedy, books, etc. Lauretta's workshop was entitled, "It's Okay to Laugh:

Humor in the Dark Places." And she knows how to deliver that worthy message.

Southern Living magazine once called her "the funniest woman in Georgia." She is a best-selling author of several books, a *Huffington Post* blogger, speaker, performer, teacher, and commentator on National Public Radio's *All Things Considered*, where her stories have reached twenty-five million listeners. Her book, *The Cracker Queen: A Memoir of a Jagged, Joyful Life*, is a poignant memoir of life on the wrong side of the tracks which includes a colorful cast of misfits, dysfunctional family members, and lessons for finding joy in spite of hardship all wrapped up in belly laughs.

So, quoting Erma Bombeck's *general* reflection, "If you can't make it better, you can laugh at it," and a page from Lauretta Hannon's How to Use Laughter in Dark Places," I certainly don't mean to marginalize the #MeToo Movement. But it means something else altogether to me when I say, "me, too." I use it when I reaffirm someone else's comment. Saying "me, too" does not just belong to the sexual misconduct movement! Let me prove my point...and with humor, of course.

Reading a friend's Facebook post last night, she said, "I make this post at 4:30 a.m. on a cold, rainy night in April. I just woke up realizing that I made a promise to attend a very important meeting. Thirty seconds after that call, I got distracted and never transferred the meeting information to my phone or refrigerator calendar. To complicate matters further, I cannot remember where the meeting was to be held or who else was to attend the meeting so that I can sincerely apologize and ask them to forgive me! I know my apology does not make up for my missing the meeting, I feel terrible. This confirms that my brain is too fried and I am too old to remember anything that I do not physically write down or put in my phone!!! #lifetoocrazy #braintoooold."

#MeToo.

But maybe to keep the first kind of #MeToo response—sexual misconduct in the workplace and beyond—from getting confused with the second kind—getting old—I could change the hashtag message and write #cantremembersh**. I am constantly misplacing my personal possessions, and when telling others about my tribulations, they confess to me they are in the same boat, which makes me feel better, just for a moment, but still makes it bittersweet that they are not only time-worn along with me but are also demonstrating the same aged conduct. I suppose I could express on Twitter another rebuttal when I am unable to find my fifth pair of reading glasses in my own home along with that hashtag. And depending on how frustrated I am, I could embellish a little more with #cantrememberjacksh**. I can think of other creative ways to express my #MeToo sentiments on aging like, #gettingoldaintforsissies #lostmymindaswellasmykeys #shouldwritethissh**down, and because I am getting ancient and forgetful, my personal favorite, #iamtoooldforthissh**.

#YouToo? Aw #sh**

A Bean Counter
vs. A Hot Tamale

*I*t's January in Georgia and it is an unusual one this year. I recently walked out of my house into twenty-four degree weather for a nail appointment…without a coat. I was hot. I am always hot. Not flashes, but a continual internal temperature set at *hot*. I am one hot mama.

After a ten-minute drive in my car without turning on the heat, I arrived. My nail technician was there on time for the first appointment of the morning. She took my hands to begin the manicure ritual and both her hands were cold. I took them in mine and said, "Let me warm you up."

I am your personal hot water bottle or your personal space heater. Come stand by me. I radiate heat. Wearing my reading glasses on top of my head like a hair band to keep my hair off my face while simultaneously keeping up with them as needed, which is all the time, I can handily retrieve them at any given moment, but because they rest on top of my head, they fog up easily. The steam permeating from the top of my head has created a vapor on the lenses, causing me to have to wipe the moisture off before I can wear them to read something. It's terrible.

Hubby is the opposite. We don't fight any longer over the thermostat in the house. In the winter, he just wears a fleece vest over his long sleeves if he's cold no matter what the season. I, on the other hand, wear short sleeves, running shorts, maybe socks or I'll be barefoot.

But in the summer?

Do you remember the 1981 movie *Body Heat*, with William Hurt and Kathleen Turner? No, no...I am not talking about that, but I am talking about how the heat can make you do strange things. Here is a hint about the movie: shyster lawyer Ned Racine (William Hurt) begins a passionate affair with Matty Walker (Kathleen Turner), wife of a wealthy Florida businessman (Richard Crenna). With the help of one of his criminal clients, bomb maker Teddy Lewis (Mickey Rourke), Ned hatches a scheme to kill Matty's husband so that they can run away together with his money.

Heat. Can make you crazy. And there were several kinds of heat in that movie, as you can imagine. My Hubby, the accountant, wanting to save money on the practical kind of heat while still trying to keep me cool, came up with the most hair-brained solutions. Oh, he was creative alright, and I was desperate so I went along with them, until I didn't.

First summer, we shut off the main floor completely and lived in the finished basement—we own a ranch with a daylight/walkout basement. Now, that doesn't sound so completely off, but since the only bedroom and bathroom downstairs were being occupied by our high school senior, he was right there all the time. Since it was temporary—just three months—we slept on the recliner and the sofa. It was very cool, but I was still miserable. This was the first of many suggestions of keeping the cost down in his dependable financial plan to minimize running the air conditioner in our Georgia summers.

When it was all over, I told him I wasn't doing that again.

So, the next summer, he let me have the upstairs again—or part of it anyway. He cut out construction foam board to enclose all of the upstairs except for the kitchen and our bedroom. The foam board was left over from use behind the drywall or something. He still had some large panels of it and cut it down to fit openings of doorways since we had several arched passageways from one room to the next. These big, beautiful Pepto Bismol pink sheets of hard foam were seen from every angle. And they did not match my kitchen colors! But I got my bathroom and my bedroom back, and my hot kitchen, where I learned a good bit more about microwave recipes those three months. The rest of the house was closed off to any cool air.

When it was all over, I told him I wasn't doing that again.

The third summer, he let me have the air back in the whole house during the day, but at night, he closed our bedroom door, again shutting off everything else in the house, but bought a single air-conditioning unit for our bedroom, which was against our HOA rules. There was not a problem with the HOA getting on to us since our master bedroom is in the back of the house and there is a big holly bush hiding it. They just didn't know about it. He installed it on my side of the bed in the window where I received bursts of cool air that sounded just like a motel's air conditioning system for their single rooms. As nice as that was for me, there is a certain smell from individual units that I don't like and I really don't like the sound of the unit increasing or decreasing the energy/sound to meet the temperature settings throughout the night.

When it was all over, I told him I wasn't doing that again.

I thought I wanted to go glamping. I may have to rethink that since I've already done it thrice. But I also wanted to stay married, so I went along to get along which is what married couples do. I gave it my best shot three times and feel I did my duty. My mama and daddy didn't put me through that. I was their only child and a princess. I told my husband that with my ascending age and who knows how much time left, I was going to be treated like royalty from here on out. No more creativity. I need cool air. Period.

So we have come to a new solution. He wants to keep the power bill down. I want to be cool. We are moving. They call it downsizing.

First Fight?

*D*ear Little Jimmy,

  In 1982, you didn't want your running buddy to get married. You thought you would lose your best golfing pal. As a bachelor, you lived in the same neighborhood and just down the street from your closest Atlanta friend. And now he was bringing his fiancée over more often and it cramped your time with him and your dual bachelor lifestyle. You decided to make sure that your buddy was certain that he was really going to go through with this wedding and marriage, so you set up your best friend and his gal for their first argument to see how it played out. I suppose you wanted to test the strength of our relationship.

As you know, Future Hubby was the guy everyone wanted at a party. He loved people. He loved social interaction. He loved bashes. He was willing to go along to get along with every kind of personality he met. He never took a stand on a controversial issue to add fuel to the drama. He allowed his male friends to posture and be the life of the party like sidekick Ed McMahon to Johnny Carson. He laughed at others' jokes while playing it safe in the background. No wonder everyone loved to have him around. He was their ready-made audience.

Your friend, an accountant, was atypical. His laugh and smile were infectious. He might be a numbers man but those numbers flew out the window at festivities, especially when alcohol was served. A very devil-may-care participant, he lived all over the United States because of his father's military career and learned how to make friends everywhere he went.

I know he told you he started playing golf at a young age and *loved* the game, and I'm sure that made you happy, because when he arrived at Auburn, he met up with you, a fraternity brother who was also on Auburn's golf team. With both of you enjoying golf so much, you became fast friends. Little Jimmy, you were his golf mentor, the one who taught him a lot of his technique. You had a special bond.

So no wonder, as a bachelor, you were upset that some new girl was going to settle in with your favorite friend. You didn't know this girl well enough to determine that you didn't like her, it was just that you were jealous, in a way, and felt threatened of her closeness with your running buddy and golfing pal of more than a decade.

I'm sure you remember this: We became engaged before Christmas in 1982. He got permission from my parents, and after their approvals, my mother gave him her mother's engagement ring for her only child to wear. There was a sort of celebration during the holidays for some friends after the announcement. Of course, you were there. Everyone was so happy for the beaming couple. But you were in the corner of the room watching intently as though spying on the engaged couple's behavior. Was this relationship real? Was there any doubt that they were meant to be together? Then, you walked up to us with your well-timed question to put us to the test. You wanted to see our response.

You knew exactly what you were doing when you asked, "Where do you two plan to spend your first Christmas?"

Boom!

Then you turned away, as quickly as a fly being shooed, without even waiting to hear the response. You dropped that bombshell, turned, and left.

Well, of course, at the same time, we both looked at each other and simultaneously answered, "With *my* family." What? This was something that had not been discussed and now the altercation began with possibly raised voices as to why one's own parents' home would be the better choice to spend one's first Christmas together.

Dearest, sweetest, Little Jimmy. You watched from afar at this scene, looking just like the Grinch who stole Christmas. You smirked from the corner of the room, enjoying the tiff and the drama.

Getting past it, you were invited to be a groomsman in the wedding. After the wedding ceremony, we shared the holidays that first year with both families. And even with that tactical challenge, Little Jimmy, we knew you cared about us and remained a close friend. We tried to see you as much as possible. But things did change. Within a year, *you* married and had children right out of the chute. With your new family, you didn't see the links all that often, either, and just ended up hitting golf balls for many years into a net in your basement.

Life moves on.

"I am *Groot!*"

*T*itle confuses you? Me, too. Most likely, if you're over forty years of age, you've never heard it. I hadn't. You might have if you are a fan of fantasy no matter what your age, but I am not. As an English teacher, I love words. Characters' names in sci-fi or fantasy are just too non-Anglican for me to grab hold and remember who they are from page to page. Supposing to be well read, you'll hardly catch me reading that genre

I'll admit to some Ray Bradbury or Kurt Vonnegut. But I'm not a fan of *Harry Potter*, *Lord of the Rings*, or *Game of Thrones*. Names from these stories just confuse me. Here are some from *Harry Potter*: Godric Gryffindor, Mafalda Hopkirk, and Salazar Slytherin. In *Lord of the Rings* you'll find: Meriadoc, Eowyn, and Denethor. While in *Games of Thrones* there are: Daenerys Targaryen, Tormund Giantsbane, and Missandei. Once names like this popped up, I was trying my best to keep up. I gave Godric the name Gordy, Meriadoc was Merridy, and Missandei was now Missy. I don't know if these characters were male or female, but I made an attempt to read these novels until about page ten.

I'm sorry. No, wait, no. I am not sorry, unless those of you reading this have those names as your given names. It's not your fault if you do. Sure, there was Beowulf and Grendel in British lit. But I didn't stay in the tenth and eleventh century all that long. I did teach it for the people who like that sort of reading. *Beowulf*, set in Scandanavia, was written by an anonymous Anglo-Saxon. Those popular books mentioned

I think are full of fantasy about their origins. I like history—non-fiction—and being absolute is something I can count on.

So, when I saw the word "Groot" and an image in the bottom corner of a video I recorded on my FB page, I was puzzled. There was this little guy, rather hard to describe he was so small, but I did see he had golden hair, he was smiling, had a hand in the air like he was waving, wore a burgundy coat and pants, and the word "Groot" written by his head with streaks of fire or either something that looked like veins protruding from the word. What was that and who put it there? I didn't know anything about such a thing.

I did what I always do. Just like in the three novels I mentioned above where I didn't remember any of the characters for this essay, I researched. I didn't even know Groot was a name yet. People my age who saw it online were asking me the same question as I was asking myself, "What is that?" Then I find that young people—Lordy, when did I start calling youthful people "young people" like my parents used to—know exactly who Groot is. Groot is a fictional superhero. He first appeared in Marvel Comics' *Guardians of the Galaxy*'s Tales to Astonish #13 (November 1960) as an extraterrestrial, sentient, tree-like creature who was an invader that intended to capture humans for experimentation.

The character was reintroduced in 2006 as a heroic, noble being and now has become a pop culture icon and internet meme with his repeated line, "I am Groot." But what does this all have to do with me? I never read these comic books nor saw the *Guardians of the Galaxy* movies. I'm only telling you because, as life-long learners, I suppose this is something we are supposed to know. I don't know why I need to know about it, but somebody thought I should and added it to my video and I *can't get it off*!

BTW—I know you know what a meme is, right?

Be Careful
What You Wish For

*M*y mother-in-law was a beauty.

As a young woman, she was tall and leggy, with dark hair and green eyes. She was in the Little Rock Junior League and was a Kappa Kappa Gamma at the University of Arkansas. A runway model, she dated the owner of Braniff Airlines before she married. Rumor had it she also went out with Lex Barker, who played Tarzan in the 1949 movie *Tarzan's Magic Fountain*. She married a handsome and well-bred Army officer who moved her around the country's Army bases with him for a fascinating life in different cities and who later retired as a lieutenant colonel.

And in her time, many women fudged on their actual age. To hold onto their youthful appearance, she and women like her fibbed a bit about how old they really were. But lies can eventually catch up with you. Although a little white lie mentioning one was just two years younger than one actually was seems like nothing, it ended up being a *grave* mistake.

My husband's family homestead, Columbia, Tennessee, is featured in the book *Majestic Middle Tennessee* by Reid Smith. This 1975 publication features homes and famous people from this area. Andrew Jackson, Davy Crockett, and President James K. Polk are likely the most well-known in this land of rolling green hills, stone walls, rail fences, and the Nashville Sound because of its close proximity to Nashville.

My husband's familial ancestral home is featured in this

book because a Revolutionary veteran was given a land grant and built this home in 1808, which still stands and is occupied by his first cousin. It is not as magnificent as other landmarks in the book, such as Belle Meade, Rattle and Snap, or Harrison House owned by the country western music star Jeannie C. Riley, but it is protected all the same by the Association for the Preservation of Tennessee Antiquities.

The property contains its own family cemetery and there have been good-natured fights at reunions for the rights of one's final resting place. My husband's father claimed a popular spot near an old shady magnolia tree.

A few years ago, my beautiful mother-in-law passed away and was laid to rest next to her husband. But here is the quandary. She lived to the ripe old real age of ninety-five. And what a milestone that really was! Shouldn't she be recognized and commended for her longevity? And yet, hadn't she told people for years that she wasn't this old?

Her oldest son, my husband's brother, handled the marker since he lived closest to this Tennessee home and forebearers' cemetery. He also designed the marker and had it placed at the head of her grave. He kept the ruse of her being younger than she was when her headstone was being designed and then engraved on the granite.

Shortly after she was interred, he kept hearing from people about what an accomplishment it was to live as long as she did as he shared the story of her real age. So, what did he do?

He did not get in touch with the company who performed the engraving service, but took the cheap route of fixing it himself soon after her demise by using a rock, or something, to scratch out the date so that it added up to ninety-five years of life. But in his stupidity, he scraped the wrong end and had her departure date overhauled. In other words, when he fixed the mistake, her date of death hadn't come to pass yet, which meant my mother-in-law was buried two years before she died.

So, instead of dead and buried…it was the other way around. And he hasn't shown his face at a family reunion since then either.

When the Stars
Aligned

What a day! I want you to tell me out of *all* these occurrences, which one *did not* happen, because I guarantee you all the rest did. There is only one fictional event. Which one is it?

1. Recently, I heard from a friend who now lives in New Hampshire. While visiting her Fayetteville, Georgia family, she wanted to have breakfast together at a certain breakfast restaurant that is not available in her state. While ordering, she asked for the five dollar menu. I had never heard of this. It was never on the table whenever I was ordering there. So my normal seven dollar breakfast now was only five dollars. And it wasn't even Senior Wednesday!

2. Afterwards, I needed to run off a pamphlet of four stories I was giving away in goodie bags to a teacher group in Georgia. Visiting a print shop, I learned the price for the three hundred copies I needed. *Wow!* Trying another print store for the same order, the difference was seventy dollars in my favor. Better. And they even did all the copying for me that I thought I was going to have to do to save money. "Come back in an hour," they said.

3. Not thinking I was going to have time to purchase

my much needed makeup on that day because I'd
be standing in front of a copier for a long while
running off copies myself, I didn't bring my
almost empty makeup bottles to have the sales
clerk identify what I usually buy. I felt sure they
would have my name and past purchases in their
system. Surprisingly, they did not, and they were
even surprised. The cosmetic rep recognized me
as I am a regular customer. I didn't recall what I
usually buy. I bring past acquisitions to reorder.
She told me that when I arrived home to look at
the names on the bottom of the products and call
the store with that information. She'd gather up all
the merchandise and set them aside for me to
come by and pick them up. Because of their
system's snafu, they would give me a ten percent
discount.

4. I then visited an all-inclusive member-card only
   warehouse. My card had expired, but to tempt me
   back, I received a gift allowance to use to shop in
   the store. Of course, I used that money toward the
   membership and was able to renew without any
   currency out of my pocket. Savings!

5. It was time for my weekly manicure-pedicure
   visit. A second location had recently become
   accessible. Curious to see their decor and
   participate in their services, the nail technician
   commented because they had recently opened,
   they were giving me a twenty percent discount.
   Yay, me!

6. Craving ham to make sandwiches over the
   weekend, I visited a deli and was placing a takeout
   order for a pound of sliced ham. The manager

walked by, saw my order, had over-ordered on their quarter hams, and offered me five times more than my order for half the price it would normally cost for that amount. What was going on?

7. Getting hungry, I wanted some drive-thru fish fillets. Normally, I just get the fillets without all the extras, take them home, and have them with some leftover vegetables. I ordered two. When I drove around to the pick-up window, and while waiting a bit for the fish to be handed over to me, the manager said they goofed on one of the fillets and were giving me a third free!

I mean, should I have played the lottery that day?

Scared to death a shoe was going to drop and void my winning streak, I picked up the waiting print order, carefully drove home, put on my pajamas, and stayed in for the rest of the evening.

Bon Voyage!

I was late to the traveling party, but once I was invited, there was no turning back. As a small town girl, I didn't even ride in an airplane until I had graduated from college. We always drove to our family excursions from Georgia. That obviously meant we didn't travel extremely far. By the time I stepped foot on that first airplane jaunt, I had only been as far west as the Mississippi River; north to Williamsburg, Virginia; east as far as Nags Head, North Carolina; and south to Daytona Beach, Florida.

Then a new adventure was waiting. When my parents retired, they finally had the time and money to spend on travel. Daddy said that after all the time at sea on a destroyer during World War II off the coast of Italy and traveling for the Chicago Cubs, he had all the travel experiences he wanted for a lifetime. So it was Mother's turn and I was the recipient of their benevolence. Where to first? Hawaii and a long San Francisco, California weekend! Later, England, Scotland, and France were among other big travel exploits. By the time I married, Hubby and I were on our way to Germany, Austria, back to France, Jamaica, the Bahamas, and Mexico. We also traveled together and separately to the four corners of the United States: Alaska. Maine. Miami, Florida. San Diego, California.

Many of these exploits were also taken with children in tow. As a Millennial, our oldest *loves* to travel! He must have gotten some of the travel bug from us. So before The Heir settles down with a wife and kids, he's spending his time and money capturing memories, and those collections include New Zealand, South Africa, Iceland, Germany, Amsterdam, Netherlands, and other far-off places in the United States.

So, what's happening now? Well, Hubby *loves* to fish and play golf, and was invited by a group of guys who rented a house at the end of the year last year to do just that in Costa Rica. He only stayed a week but we certainly encouraged him to go with all that deep sea fishing they are known for and their plush golf courses. The "Where's Waldo" son? During Christmas 2017, he toured China while visiting a friend teaching English as a second language.

But I think I have the best upcoming trip, and it will be my first time there. Celebrities such as Phil Donahue, Dave Barry, Art Buchwald, Amy Ephron, and Roy Blount Jr. have been there. This year, an award-winning cartoonist with *The New Yorker* magazine, author, and editor will be advising participants. An Emmy Award-winning comedy writer for *Roseanne*, *Mad About You*, *Veronica's Closet*, and head writer for the #1 children's animated series *Rugrats* will be encouraging the attendees. The special guest this year will be John Grogan, author of the international #1 bestseller *Marley & Me: Life and Love with the World's Worst Dog*. I'll be staying in a plush Marriott and be the recipient of wonderful meals. Being among a selective few other humorists, and only occurring every other year, I will be learning and laughing my head off April 5-8 at the Erma Bombeck Writer's Workshop, which is the only one in the country devoted to both humor and human interest writing. Their motto? "You're guaranteed to laugh. A lot." Where will it be? In beautiful downtown Dayton, Ohio! Bon voyage!

The Author

Lee St. John is an unapologetic rogue Southern Belle, high-jinx expert, and mayhem confessor. With all the cotillion classes and etiquette lessons, you'd think she'd know how to behave better, yet she's merciless when she speaks her mind, ratting out former presidents of the United States, the mafia, an Augusta Master's winner, a Super Bowl Champion quarterback, famous personalities, dead people, and everyone else she knows, *including* her family and friends. To Lee, everyone is fair game because she also rats out herself. As a storyteller, she has been compared to family funny woman Erma Bombeck, but with an edge; Southern humorist, Lewis Grizzard, but with PG-13 rated twists; genuine tell-all, Ali Wentworth, fearlessly describing her secrets; and any frisky *Seinfeld* episode—especially when George is involved. Betcha thought she'd say Elaine. Since high school, she has had her own newspaper columns and was told once by a publisher she should write a book. Majoring in journalism and mass communications, her first job after college graduation was with a national advertising agency. Think *Mad Men*. Later attending graduate school in English education, she taught every grade but first. A Georgia Peach, Lee St. John has been married to her Southern gentleman for 35 years. They have two Millennial sons and a tater-tot-looking Schnauzer, OBie.

 **Connect**
With Me

Facebook: https://www.facebook.com/leestjohnauthor
Instagram: https://instagram.com/leestjohnauthor/
Website and Blog: http://www.leestjohnauthor.com/
Twitter: @LeeStJohnauthor
Newspaper: Newnan Times-Herald Contributor (Ga.),
Fayette-News
Contributor (Fayetteville, Ga.)
Radio: WQEE 99.1 FM HOST of "Spilling the Beans Book
Club"/Live on FB
Pinterest: LeeStJohnAuthor
https://www.goodreads.com/author/show/14343509.Lee_St_J
ohn/blog

A member of:
National Society of Newspaper Columnists
Atlanta Writers Club
Humorous Writers of America
Southern Living Magazine THE FRONT PORCH Board

Can be found on Amazon.com

f facebook.com/leestjohnauthor

⊙ instagram.com/leestjohnauthor

53979414R00159

Made in the USA
Columbia, SC
25 March 2019